Mongrel Nation

Jeffersonian America

EDITORS
Jan Ellen Lewis
Peter S. Onuf
Andrew O'Shaughnessy

Mongrel Nation

The America Begotten
by Thomas Jefferson
and Sally Hemings

Clarence E. Walker

University of Virginia Press

Charlottesville & London

University of Virginia Press
© 2010 by the Rector and Visitors
of the University of Virginia
All rights reserved
Printed in the United States of America
on acid-free paper

First published 2009
First paperback edition published 2010
ISBN 978-0-8139-2778-7 (paper)

9 8 7 6 5 4 3 2 1

The Library of Congress has cataloged the
hardcover edition as follows:

Library of Congress Cataloging-in-Publication Data
Walker, Clarence Earl.
    Mongrel nation : the America begotten by Thomas
Jefferson and Sally Hemings / Clarence E. Walker.
    p. cm. — (Jeffersonian America)
Includes bibliographical references and index.
ISBN 978-0-8139-2777-0 (cloth : alk. paper)
    1. Miscegenation — United States — History.
2. United States — Race relations.   3. Jefferson,
Thomas, 1743–1826 — Relations with women.
4. Jefferson, Thomas, 1743–1826 — Relations with
slaves.   5. Hemings, Sally.   6. Whites — Race
identity — United States.   7. African Americans
— Race identity.   8. Racially mixed people —
United States.   I. Title.
E185.62.W35 2009
306.84'60973 — dc22   2008024042

For Winthrop D. Jordan
and Leon Litwack

We were integrated in the womb.

—James Baldwin

Slavery . . . was not the whips and chains of the
school history books, not the breaking apart of
families or the unending driving labor but some
stain far greater and deeper, something that had
been unleashed and then bloomed up, between
and within at once both races, white and black,
forever without surcease, tenacious, untouchable
and unchangeable.

—Jeffrey Lent

. . . swingin' white dick hot for black poon.

—Philip Roth

Look at the so-called whites, who've left bastards
all over the known earth.

It's easy for a Negroe to "pass" for white. . . .
I don't think it would be so simple for a white
person to "pass" for coloured.

—Nella Larsen

Contents

Acknowledgments

WRITING IS ALWAYS a lonely and difficult process, and the task is even more stressful when one is in pain. From 2003 to 2005, as I was working on early drafts of this book, I suffered from extreme arthritis in both hips. I have now had two hip replacements and feel like I am nineteen from the hips down. I first of all want to thank my surgeon and all of my friends for seeing me through this time of trial.

The following friends and colleagues talked with me about this project, made suggestions and corrections, and encouraged me while I was writing. First, I would like to thank Peter Onuf, known to some as "the master puppeteer of uppity Negroes." Peter has been a wonderful critic and supporter of my work, and his humor and enormous knowledge of the Jeffersonian world have been invaluable to me while writing this project. I also want to thank Jan Ellen Lewis, whose article "The White Jeffersons" taught me a great deal about family and family secrets. Another important influence has been the pioneering and brilliant scholarship of Annette Gordon-Reed, whose book sparked a great discussion in my seminar, as in the scholarly world at large, on the question of national identity. Annette, like the late Thelma Willis Foote, has had an impact on how I think about the writing of American history and the place of black people in the American past.

Second, the following group of historians and friends, over meals, drinks, and long phone conversations, played an important role in the writing of this book: Henry Abelove, Robert Abzug, Emily Albu, Robert Aldrich, Glenn Altschuler, David Blight, Henrik Bodker,

Brian Connolly, Robin Einhorn, Joanne Freeman, Harris Friedberg, Susan Glenn, Norman Kutcher, Daniel Littlefield, Valinda Littlefield, Mel McCombie, Richard Mendoza, Dirk Moses, Bruce Poch, Fernando Purcell, Andres Resendez, Rosalind Rosenberg, Nick Salvatore, Mike Sherry, Richard Slotkin, Valerie Smith, Jennifer Spear, Blake Stimson, and John Sweet. At Davis I have benefited enormously from conversations with Joanne Diehl, Omnia El Shakry, Karen Halttunen, Clarence Major, Lisa Materson, Riche Richardson, Sudipta Sen, John Smolenski, Alan Taylor, and David Van Leer. I would also like to thank Kate Gilbert for critically reading the manuscript and teaching me that commas are important. A great debt of thanks is owed to my editor, Richard Holway, the history and social sciences editor of the University of Virginia Press, who waited patiently for this little book. It has been my great pleasure at Davis to work with graduate students in the American history and cultural studies PhD programs. So I would like to thank David Barber, Brian Behnken, Barbara Ceptus, Ruma Chopra, Kelly Hopkins, Iris Jerkes, Kathy Littles, Louis Moore, and Gregory Smithers, whose forthcoming work on comparative miscegenation in Australia and the United States has been invaluable for understanding how unexceptional the United States is.

Finally, this book is dedicated to my two favorite teachers in graduate school, the late Winthrop D. Jordan and Leon F. Litwack. Together they were two of the most important historians of their generation. At Berkeley in the sixties, History 167A and 167B were two of the most popular course offerings in the history curriculum. Both of these men were inspiring teachers — thoughtful, kind, and generous to their students. I have often asked myself, after leaving Berkeley, how these two white men put up with my ironic and contrarian sensibility.

Mongrel Nation

Introduction

THE THOMAS JEFFERSON–SALLY HEMINGS affair has been an issue in American political, social, cultural, and racial life since 1802, when James Thompson Callender, a transplanted Scottish newspaperman living in Virginia, published a story in the *Richmond Recorder* accusing Jefferson of being Sally Hemings's lover and the father of children she bore after returning to the United States from a sojourn in Paris. Given that the sexual exploitation of female slaves has always been an integral part of all slave systems, Callender's accusation thus placed Jefferson squarely in a tradition of master-slave relations that dates back to ancient times.

Callender has been called a muckraker and described as a "misshapen little man who made a career of spewing venom."[1] I do not doubt that Callender was an unpleasant character, but in making public Jefferson's relationship with his slave Sally Hemings he nevertheless performed a public service. His revelation showed that Jefferson was a more complex white supremacist than was suggested by query 14 of his *Notes on the State of Virginia,* in which he disparaged the physical and mental characteristics of black people.

Some have concluded on the basis of this and other published writings that Jefferson would never have slept with a black woman. Callender's suggestion that Jefferson was an "amalgamationist" was, and is, thus anathema to Jefferson's partisans, to whom the charge has been both libelous and politically motivated. It should not be forgotten that Jefferson had political enemies, and in a racial state, in which whiteness was and continues to be both a fetish and an icon, what better way to wound a prominent white politician than to accuse him of sleeping with a black woman? Regardless of Callender's motivation, however, the reaction to his revelation illuminates the great discomfiture of some white Americans, past and present, when forced to contemplate Jefferson's relationship with Sally Hemings. The importance of Callender's exposé resides above all in the reactions it has evoked in Jefferson's political allies, members of his family, historians, and modern Jefferson apologists.[2]

The Jefferson-Hemings affair, given Jefferson's place in the pantheon of the Founding Fathers, raises questions about the national identity or racial provenance of the United States. Using it as a point of departure, I want to posit in this book a new myth of origin of the United States. That is, I am suggesting that at the moment of its creation the nation was not a white racial space but a mixed-race one, in which Jefferson and Hemings, as a mixed-race couple, rather than George and Martha Washington, should be considered the founding parents of the North American republic.

I realize that this may be disturbing to some, and particularly to my peers in American colonial history, but studies of other colonial settler societies indicate that they began as racially creolized societies. Why is the United States regarded as an exception to this rule? The answer to this question may lie in an earlier generation of American historians' conception of America as a white nation and their deification of Jefferson as the apotheosis of white manhood. It may also reside in some white Americans' unease about interracial sex and its role in the creation of the American people. In brief, the attitude of some white Americans toward the very idea of a liaison between Jefferson and Hemings, ambivalent at best and more often deeply hostile and resistant, is representative of a congenital racial tension in American society.

Examples of this disquiet about the third president of the republic and his slave concubine can be seen in the public's and the historical profession's responses to several rounds of discussion in the past half-century about the Jefferson-Hemings affair. First, Winthrop Jordan's examination of Thomas Jefferson and Sally Hemings in his book *White over Black* (1968) presented a provocative analysis of Jefferson, Hemings, slavery, and race. Although he did not embrace Callender, Jordan did note that the president was present at Monticello nine months before each of his bondwoman's children was born. Jordan wrote that "Jefferson's paternity can be neither refuted nor proved from the known circumstances or from the extant testimony of his overseer, his white descendants or the descendants of Sally, each of them having fallible memories and personal interest at stake."[3] Jordan's work has to be placed in the broader context of the change in American attitudes about race, sex, and sexuality that began during the 1950s and flourished in the 1960s.[4] By the 1960s all kinds of sex and sexuality that had been unthinkable in 1950 were beginning to be talked about and practiced.[5] The book also reflected the fact that because of the civil rights movement, some black and white Americans were becoming more tolerant of interracial sex. I do not want to suggest that *White over Black* settled the issue of Jefferson and Hemings in American history or, for that matter, the place of interracial sex in our nation's past. Instead, it initiated a conversation between women (black and white) and the white-male-dominated American historical profession about a Founding Father's sexuality.

Historians do not change their ideas easily, especially not when the subject is a man like Thomas Jefferson, whose name is synonymous with America. This can be seen in the historical profession's response to the biographer Fawn Brodie's *Thomas Jefferson: An Intimate History* (1974) and the novel *Sally Hemings* (1979), by the black novelist Barbara Chase-Riboud.[6] Both works were inspired by the second wave of feminism. Chase-Riboud's novel, built upon the premise that the relationship between Jefferson and Hemings was ultimately a love affair, was criticized and denounced as "an angry polemic."[7] Brodie's biography provoked intense debate among professional historians because it stated without qualification what Winthrop Jordan was only willing to accept as a possibility: that Callender's accusation was accurate and that Madison Hemings, Sally Hemings's second male child, was correct in identifying Jefferson as his father.[8]

Prior to the publication of her biography, Brodie unleashed a debate at a meeting of the Organization of American Historians in April 1971 when she presented a paper titled "The Great Jefferson Taboo." According to Scot French and Edward Ayers, Merrill Peterson "was critical of the psychological evidence presented by Brodie."[9] Winthrop Jordan, on the other hand, "stated that he had already been sixty percent on what might be called the Brodie side of the argument and described himself as having upped the percentage to eighty after reading her paper. He was impressed with the psychological evidence."[10] The debate continued after Brodie published her paper as an article in *American Heritage* magazine in 1972 and intensified with the publication of the biography itself two years later.

Although Brodie's book was a huge popular success, it received mixed reviews from historians and literary critics. One of the most strident of these was Garry Wills, who savaged Brodie's interpretation of Jefferson and Hemings's relationship in the *New York Review of Books*. "Some," Wills said, "will find this picture of Thomas Jefferson unattractive — but Ms. Brodie proves that the attempt to construct one more to the liking of today's romantic day dreamers involves heroic feats of misunderstanding and a constant labor at ignorance. This seems too high a price to pay when the same appetites can be more readily gratified by those Hollywood fan magazines, with their wealth of unfounded conjecture on the sex lives of others, from which Ms. Brodie has borrowed her scholarly methods." Wills's hostility to Brodie also extended to her subject Sally Hemings. "She was like a healthy and obliging prostitute," he wrote, "who could be suitably rewarded but would make no importunate demands."[11]

When the debate resurfaced in the 1990s, it reflected the growing willingness of black scholars to question the prevailing belief that Thomas Jefferson and Sally Hemings were not intimate. This black intellectual self-assertion was part of the blowback of the civil rights movement and reflected an ongoing black intellectual impatience with white cultural presumption. In 1997 the brilliant legal and historical critic Annette Gordon-Reed published *Thomas Jefferson and Sally Hemings: An American Controversy*. Gordon-Reed's book argued that both Callender and black testimony should be taken seriously. The fact that Thomas Jefferson was present at Monticello nine months before each of Hemings's children was born, Gordon-Reed said, was a reason to rethink the entire matter.

In the year following the publication of Gordon-Reed's book, 1998, an article appeared in the journal *Nature* claiming on the basis of DNA evidence that Thomas Jefferson was the father of Sally Hemings's last child, Eston Hemings. This, as Peter Onuf and Jan Lewis have argued, was "news and no news at all."[12] It was no news to black people, who had grown up with an oral history of miscegenation, a legacy of stories that contextualized the black understanding not only of American history but also of the nation's racial and sexual mores. In demonstrating a genetic link between Eston Hemings and the male Jeffersons, however, science had now provided a connection between Jefferson and Hemings that Jefferson apologists would find difficult to explain away as mere speculation or hearsay.

This book is an intervention in the debates about the Thomas Jefferson–Sally Hemings affair. Readers familiar with this subject will see my indebtedness to Andrew Burstein, Jan Lewis, Peter Onuf, Annette Gordon-Reed, Joshua Rothman, and John Sweet, to name some of the scholars who have influenced my thinking about race and nation.[13] This work builds on, but also moves in a different direction from, the scholarship previously cited. I agree with those scholars who have argued that Thomas Jefferson was the father of Sally Hemings's children. The preponderance of the evidence — the timing of Thomas Jefferson's visits to Monticello, the birth dates of Sally Hemings's children, the DNA evidence, and the sexual world Jefferson grew up in — leads me to agree with my peers. But here I wish to broaden our understanding by situating the relationship in a larger, world context.

First, I place the Jefferson-Hemings relationship in the context of what Philip Curtin called the "plantation complex,"[14] namely, the plantations of the Caribbean and North and South America, which were "brought into existence by Europe's powerful and seemingly limitless appetite for their products."[15] The slave systems developed in the plantation complex "embodied a new type of slavery," and wherever plantations were located, "African captives and their descendants . . . replaced or were soon to replace Indian slaves or European indentured servants as the principal labour force."[16] I argue that when perceived from this perspective, the relationship between Jefferson and Hemings was neither unusual nor exceptional in terms of master-slave sexuality in the New World or, for that matter, in world history. In brief, we have to abandon the idea of an American exceptionalism when dealing with Jefferson and Hemings.

American exceptionalism has always had a racial subtext. Perfect at its creation, according to the myth, America escaped the social processes — amalgamation/miscegenation — that characterized other colonial settler societies. I understand that America was not Australia, Brazil, Cuba, or South Africa in the seventeenth century, but in its early history it intersected with these societies on the issue of interracial sexuality. Jefferson and Hemings were not social isolates but participants in a process of race making that was international in scope. When placed in a "world context and over centuries, the mixing of peoples of different colors and features that occurred in America was, of course, but a continuation of a process that is practically as old as the history of mankind," Joel Williamson noted.[17] Whites and blacks had been copulating and producing children in Africa, Europe, and Asia long before Columbus bumped into the wrong land mass on his way to the East.

In Latin America the process of racial intermixture began a century before Virginia was settled. Thus, depending on their place of origin, some blacks who arrived in North America in the seventeenth century were not purely Negroid. They were, as Ira Berlin has recently suggested, creolized both culturally and biologically.[18] This was particularly true of blacks who came from the West Indies, where whites and blacks created what Winthrop Jordan has called a "chiaroscuro of races."[19] Only in the United States did this form of social interaction become a "closeted" aspect of national history, something to be denied rather than affirmed. In a society obsessed with whiteness, there could be no derogation of that color. Sexual encounters between whites and blacks were constructed as offenses against whiteness. As early as 1662 in Virginia, a law was passed in reaction to interracial sex, according to Richard Hofstadter.[20]

In focusing on black and white in this essay, I do not mean to give the impression that race in America has always been reducible to that binarism. Quite the opposite. But historically the central tension in American history has been between these two groups. The Jefferson-Hemings liaison is one of the issues that sits at the heart of what I refer to as the racial tension between black and white Americans.

White North American unease about interracial sex was evident at a conference in which I participated at the University of Richmond seven years ago called "Thomas Jefferson and Sally Hemings: Discovering and Dealing with the Truth."[21] The proceedings had barely begun when a white man, later identified as a member of the local chapter of the Klan, objected to a number of the participants. He called the panel "politically correct," an oblique reference to the fact that seven of the eleven panelists were black. According to our critic, we had come to Richmond solely to besmirch the reputation of a great man. There could be no other reason, he said, because it was self-evident that Jefferson had not done what the DNA evidence suggested. To prove this point, the Klansman asked the panelists if we had read Jefferson's *Notes on the State of Virginia*. When we replied that we had, we were told that Jefferson's derogation of black people in that book was proof positive that he could not have had an affair with a black woman. What people write and what they do in their private lives, however, are two separate things. No understanding of Jefferson based on his published work can comprehend the complexity of his racial and sexual life. Before this incident is dismissed as marginal or insignificant, I would suggest that skeptics consult the ongoing discussion on the Internet of the 1998 *Nature* article.

We cannot comprehend Jefferson's relationship with Hemings if it is seen solely as a case of "carrot-top raping a black woman," as one of my former white female graduate students used to call it. Just what the internal dynamics of this affair were we will never know, but I think that to call it rape is simplistic. The affair, which lasted thirty-eight years, was like long-term relationships between masters and female slaves in the Caribbean and Brazil, in which the parties seem to have negotiated some form of sexual modus vivendi.

Nor has this relationship produced in black America the same response that Hernán Cortés's affair with the enslaved Indian princess Malinche created in Mexican and Chicano history.[22] No one in black American history has given Hemings a nickname like the one given to Malinche: "La Chingada" (literally, "The Screwed One").[23] The dual senses of victimhood and racial or national betrayal embodied in this characterization of Malinche are not part of the black American understanding of Sally Hemings's relationship with Thomas Jefferson. In retrospect, their affair has been viewed by black Americans since the nineteenth century as complicating an American past often rendered in simplistic terms, one in which the relationship of black people to the founders and creation of the republic has been largely ignored.[24]

Finally, this project is about who owns history. Is our understanding of the American past to be forever shaped by white male historians, as it has been for most of American history, or will the voices of other men and women be integrated into the canon of American history rather than dismissed as political correctness or special pleading? Personally, I do not think that the complicated racial and sexual past of America can be denied any longer. This book is an effort to correct that understanding.

One | Sexuality

MY PURPOSE in this chapter is to place the affair of Thomas Jefferson and Sally Hemings in the broader context of what Philip D. Curtin terms the "plantation complex."[1] When viewed from this perspective, the relationship was neither unusual nor aberrant, but normative. Sex between men of the master class or race and their slaves has always been a given in both "societies with slaves and slave societies."[2] I also want to suggest an alternative reading of female slave sexuality that moves beyond the idea of Hemings as a victim of rape. Not all sexual encounters between black slave women and white men were rapes. In a world where there was no such thing as consensual sex, the relationship between Thomas Jefferson and Sally Hemings can be located on a continuum of sexual practices. Historians of sexuality and slavery must move beyond the idea propounded by Havelock Ellis that sexuality can be understood, as Jeffrey Weeks observed, "in terms of neat categories and typologies." "Sexuality as presented and sexuality as lived," Weeks wrote, "always overflows the common-sense knowledge that people, including historians, have imposed on it."[3]

Wherever European males went during the fifteenth century and afterward, they created new societies and peoples by mating with women from subject populations.[4] Interracial sexual relationships (often termed *miscegenation* today and *amalgamation* before 1864) were common in the Dutch, English, French, Portuguese, and Spanish colonial possessions.[5] The peoples produced by these unions were treated in varying ways by their European conquerors. On the whole, Protestants were more troubled than Catholics by the process of racial intermixture, as a number of studies of amalgamation/miscegenation have shown. Portugal is emblematic of one of the more racially relaxed colonial powers. Writing about the seventeenth century, the Portuguese historian Antonio de Oliveira Cadornega, author of the *Historia General das Guerras Angolanas* (General History of the Angolan Wars), observed, "The soldiers of the garrison and other European individuals father many children on the black ladies, for want of white ladies, with the result that there are many Mulattoes and Coloureds *(pardos).*" The process of interracial mating in Portuguese colonies began before the sixteenth century, wrote Cadornega, when some of the Portuguese in the Senegambia "were able to marry into the ruling families." This form of interaction was also common in the Congo, where "for many decades [the Portuguese] mixed amicably with the Congolese in general and mated freely with the women in particular."[6] Crossing the Atlantic, the Portuguese, "being in want of wives, whereby to propagate their virtues," said Cadornega, "took to themselves Indians and Negresses" in São Paulo, Brazil.[7] Commenting in the second quarter of the sixteenth century on the ubiquity of interracial sex on the island of São Tomé, a Portuguese pilot offhandedly observed, "They all have wives and children, and some of the children who are born there are as white as ours."[8] Within São Paulo, "the vast majority of women with whom the old Paulistas mated were Indians, if only because they could not afford to buy Negresses. This mixed Luso-Indian race formed the bulk of the population in the southern captaincies by 1614."[9] In the provinces of Bahia and Pernambuco, on the other hand, mulattoes predominated because of a vast "importation" of black slaves.[10]

Sex across the color line was no less widespread in Britain's North American colonies. Yet for the British, interracial sex came to be a major source of social unease. Within the British colonies of the Americas, only in the West Indies were the social and cultural proscriptions of interracial sex publicly flouted. Writing in the 1770s, Edward Long, the historian of Jamaica, described racial amalgamation there with a distaste that was heightened by his perception of race mixing in the Spanish colonies of the New World. In the Spanish empire, Long saw a more developed version of the "degeneracy" unfolding in the English colony of Jamaica, where he lived. Long asked his readers to turn their "eyes to the Spanish dominions and behold what a vicious, brutal, and degenerate breed of mongrels [has] been there produced, between Spaniards, Blacks, Indians, and their mixed progeny. . . . [His readers] must be of the opinion, that it might be much better for Britain, and Jamaica too, if the white men in the colony would abate of their infatuated attachments to black women."[11] Commenting on the lewdness of Jamaican planters and of white males generally, Long wrote that "not one in twenty can be persuaded, that there is either sin or shame in cohabiting with his slave." Equally disturbing to Long was the fact that these unions "usher into the world a train of tarnished beings," that is, of people of mixed racial origin.[12] The creation of these human beings was accompanied by the birth of a vocabulary that attempted to place people between the fictive poles of white and black.

In all of the European colonies of the New World the "classificatory calculus" of *mulatto, quadroon,* and *octoroon* provided racial markers for establishing a person's distance from whiteness. The "mathematics of blood" involved in the creation of racial types defined as one-half, one-fourth, or one-eighth Negro emerged "from a single racist theorem," according to the literary critic Lee Edelman, who went on to add that "wherever an admixture of 'black blood' is at issue, one part determines the whole."[13] Racial mixing "called into question the criteria by which Europeaness [*sic*] could be identified, citizenship accorded, and nationality assigned" in the United States until the passage of the Fourteenth Amendment in 1868.[14] The creation of mixed-race offspring who were white or nearly white in the English colonies and what later became the United States exacerbated the unease European Americans have always had about "the solidity of American national identity [and the] need to protect that identity,"[15] beginning with the Age of Exploration and settlement and continuing, I would maintain, to the present day.

Whiteness as a necessary condition of citizenship was enshrined in some of the earliest documents of the republic. One of these was the Naturalization Act of 1790, by which Congress stipulated that "any alien, being a free white person, who shall have resided within the limits and under the jurisdiction of the United States for the term of two years, may be admitted to become a citizen thereof." Eleven years earlier, Thomas Jefferson had authored a bill limiting citizenship in the Commonwealth of Virginia to "white persons" who met certain other criteria.[16] And as Leon Litwack has pointed out, citizenship was not the only thing limited to whites. Service in the military became a prerogative of white males in 1792, blacks were excluded from carrying the mail in 1810, and in 1820 the citizens of Washington, D.C., were authorized to elect white officials and instructed to adopt a code that restricted the freedoms of free Negroes and slaves.[17]

The fact that the United States, like Australia, Germany, Japan, and South Africa, constructed itself from the outset as a racial state has had a profound effect on how we understand the racial origins of the American republic. The philosopher David Theo Goldberg defines racial states in these terms: "States are racial more deeply because of the structural position they occupy in producing and reproducing, constituting racially shaped spaces and places, groups and events, life worlds and possibilities, access and restrictions, inclusions and exclusions, conceptions and modes of representations."[18] Another useful term for thinking about this country's racial origins, *Herrenvolk Democracy,* is popular with a number of American historians, myself included. Most famously associated with the work of Pierre L. van den Berghe, the term refers to a society divided between citizens with full rights and noncitizens with no rights in which the distinction between the two is racially based. The concept of the United States as Herrenvolk Democracy, while useful, now needs to be extended back to the seventeenth and eighteenth centuries. What we call the United States constituted itself as a white racial space much earlier than Jefferson's 1779 bill and the immigration law of 1790 indicate, and certainly earlier than several recent studies of whiteness suggest.[19] Indeed, the idea of America as a democracy was constructed in opposition to blackness.

For the Founding Fathers, including Jefferson, the American republic was created with blacks as either de jure or de facto outsiders.[20] To be black was a sign of American inauthenticity. The political scientist Rogers Smith insightfully captured the problematic status of blacks in the Jeffersonian republic when he wrote:

> The presence in the nation's political culture of well established arguments for the divine mission of the American people, the superiority of Anglo-Saxon civilization, patriarchal rule in the family and polity, and white racial supremacy all not only permitted white Christian men of the Jeffersonian age to be proud, rather than apologetic, about their possession of full citizenship. As much or more than the Declaration of Independence, those notions defined the meaning of the American nation whose interest had to be advanced. They made acceptance of the equality of those who did not share these traits seem a betrayal of shared values, not a fulfillment of liberal justice.[21]

Being black has thus transhistorically operated as a negative reference point for white Americans, in that it has told them not only who they were and were not but also what they did not want to become. The presence of blacks, whether free or slave, both in colonial society and later in the republic, undermined the idea that America was a community solely comprised of white people.

Although blacks were not citizens of the nation, their presence in America had a profound impact on the society's culture and politics. Even before the creation of the American republic, the abolitionist Samuel Sewall, who expressed a great deal of sympathy for enslaved blacks in his 1700 pamphlet *The Selling of Joseph: A Memorial,* argued for an all-white colony of Massachusetts. Sewall thought white servants in Massachusetts "would conduce more to the Welfare of the Province . . . for a term of Years, than to have Slaves for Life." Whites, Sewall claimed, could not "endure to hear of a Negro's being made free," and once free, blacks "seldom [used] their freedom well." Blacks continued to aspire "after their forbidden Liberty," and once they were free, there was "such a disparity in their Conditions, Color & Hair, that they can never embody with us, and grow up into orderly Families, to the Peopling of the Land." The problem with blacks was that they would exist in the Massachusetts "Body Politick as a kind of extravasat Blood."[22] Unlike white blood, black blood was not normal, but bruised, and thus it posed a threat to white society.

Sewall's concern about the contamination that would result from the amalgamation of black and white was not an isolated anxiety confined solely to North America. Unease about the future of whiteness can also be found in other British colonial settler societies. Sudipta Sen has brilliantly adumbrated similar concerns in eighteenth- and nineteenth-century India, where the British administrators of the colony were fearful of the consequences of amalgamation with the subcontinent's indigenous population.[23] In North America, Sewall's disquiet about the place of "colored people" in the nation surfaced again in the debates about the territories acquired as a result of the Mexican War. Echoes of Sewall's fears about America's whiteness can be found in the 1840s comments of South Carolina senator John C. Calhoun, who gave voice to the sentiment that America was a white nation when he opposed the annexation of Mexico's former western provinces on the grounds that "we have never dreamt of incorporating into our Union any but the Caucasian race — the free white race."[24] Calhoun's use of the words *Caucasian, incorporating,* and *union* reflects a discomfort about assimilating a people who were a mixture of black, Native American, and Spanish, in both a political and a physical and sexual sense, and thus it mirrors a Jeffersonian unease about blackness and certain types of hybrids. Calhoun's anxiety about the racial provenance of Mexicans was also shared by Stephen Austin, a future president of the Republic of Texas, who said that Texas's struggle with Mexico was "a war of barbarism and of despotic principles, waged by the mongrel Spanish-Indian and Negro race, against civilization and the Anglo-American Race."[25] This anxiety about mixed-race people carried over into the twentieth century; in 1912, for example, Congressman Seaborn Roddenberg of Georgia told the House of Representatives that he favored passage of a law that would "prevent white women from being corrupted by a strain of kinky-headed blood."[26]

All of the preceding is intended to indicate that I think of the history of the American republic as a racial history. The genocidal dispossession of the Native American, the enslavement and "Jim Crowing" of blacks, the invasion of Mexico and the colonization of Mexicans, the exclusion of Asians, and the racialization of various white ethnic groups suggest that historically the United States has been a society obsessed with race and racism. Furthermore, this obsession with race has not produced a "*single* invariant racism but a number of *racisms,* forming a broad, open spectrum of situations."[27]

In focusing my discussion on race, I do not mean to ignore class and class struggle as factors in American history. Nevertheless, as the German historical anthropologist Verena Martinez-Alier has pointed out, "In the United States . . . the 'visibility' of racial distinctions — a legacy from slavery — endows race with a degree of autonomy as a source of discrimination that obscures class as its ultimate root."[28] To focus on class also ignores the fact that both white and nonwhite Americans transhistorically have been objectified beyond their class position. From this perspective, a class analysis obscures the history of race and racism in the United States. The histories of Asians, blacks, Mexicans, and Native Americans have not been lived as equivalent either to one another or to the history of white Americans, even when they have occupied the same class position. This is clear, for example, in the history of slavery in seventeenth-century Chesapeake, where blacks replaced Native Americans as slaves and replaced whites as indentured servants. Where the pasts of Asians, blacks, Mexicans, and Native Americans intersect in American history is in the Euro-American perception that all of these groups have, at various moments in the nation's history, been defined as "others within" the nation.[29] Specifically for blacks in the United States this has meant that they "physically reside within the nation yet remain psychically other to the nation."[30]

The psychological and physical alterity of blacks in American society is deeply grounded in a Jeffersonian revulsion to blackness that was both psychic and physical, as his correspondence and the *Notes on the State of Virginia* indicate. Commenting on Jefferson's antipathy to blacks, Andrew Burstein recently noted that "Jefferson's racism made dark pigmentation into something repellent."[31] Jefferson did not, to paraphrase Burstein, invent the category of "white racial conceit," that is, whiteness as an iconicized and fetishized sign of beauty, with blackness being its antithesis.[32] The idealization of whiteness began long before the rise of Christianity and thus long before the creation of the United States in the eighteenth century.[33] But Thomas Jefferson was a man of the Enlightenment, a period in which "beauty was linked to the desire for procreation."[34] Jefferson, as his writings indicate, was concerned with the issue of procreation because he thought that if a republic was

to survive, it had to have a harmonious and homoge
tion. The presence of both black and white people in
their propensity to mix thus posed a threat to the n
as a white racial state. Jefferson's obsession with the
place of blacks in American society suggests that on s
did not think the United States was a nation as long as
present within its boundaries. If whites were a distinct "people,"
what would their future be if they cohabited with blacks?[35]

Jefferson's answer to this problem, as Peter Onuf has written,
was to create a "secure sexual frontier" between two peoples (black
and white).[36] This was a variation on an idea conceptualized by the
German philosopher Johann Gottlieb Fichte, who, in a different
context, wrote of "interior frontiers." The idea of an "interior frontier" or a "secure sexual frontier" is interesting because of its "con-
tradictory connotations," according to Laura Stoler. It is a "site of
both enclosure and contact, of observed passage and exchange."[37]
When Fichte's and Jefferson's concerns about frontier are read as a
metaphorical anxiety about interracial sex, they speak to a deeply
ingrained fear that both white Americans and Germans have had
about race, national purity, and identity.[38] If the nation was an or-
ganism, this thinking went, it had to be protected against decay and
degeneration. For Jefferson, this meant sealing whites off from contact with blacks. His solution to the problem of the "deep-rooted
prejudices" that whites entertained toward blacks was to send
blacks out of the country.[39]

Writing to James Monroe, governor of Virginia, on 24 November 1801, Jefferson recommended resettling blacks outside of the
continental United States. "The West Indies," Jefferson wrote,
"offer a more probable & practicable retreat for them. Inhabited
already by a people of their own race & color; climates congenial
with their natural constitution; insulated from other descriptions
of men; nature seems to have formed these islands to become the

acle of the blacks transplanted into this hemisphere." If the .est Indies proved to be unavailable, Jefferson continued, "Africa would offer a last & undoubted resort."[40]

Whatever their ultimate destination, Jefferson favored expelling blacks so that they would not confound the progress of his beloved republic. "The Empire for Liberty," John Murrin has written, was "for whites only."[41] Although Jefferson's call for the colonization of blacks preceded the organization of the American Colonization Society in 1816, it formed part of the postrevolutionary move toward creation of a white republic — that period of American history, stretching roughly from 1790 to 1820, that saw a slow and gradual contraction of the freedom blacks thought they had acquired as a result of the revolution.[42] David Waldstreicher has described this process as an "attempt to render America unmixed."[43] For Jefferson, the political and social body of America was white; this perception was embedded in his thought about both political and cultural meaning long before the rise of scientific racism. Jefferson's white-supremacist championing of a democratic culture can be seen in his understanding of the impact of slavery on Virginia and the South generally. Jefferson's antipathy to slavery did not arise out of a concern for blacks; he opposed slavery because it corrupted whites. Writing about the master-slave relationship, Jefferson said that black bondage had an "unhappy influence on the manners of our people produced by the existence of slavery among us."[44]

Black people understood what underlay this type of thinking and how it corrupted the ideal of democracy. Commenting on the state of American democracy in 1837, the black newspaper *Colored American* observed that "the democratic principle is adopted in America where the rich and poor, the high and low could all come together as equals to hate the colored man."[45] What the paper describes is a racism that functions as what the Germans dubbed an *Integrationsideologie,* an ideology capable of uniting a wide spectrum of social groups that might have been hostile to one another at various times but would coalesce in antiblack racism.[46]

The placement of race at the center of American history explains the hysteria and denial surrounding the 1998 revelation that Jefferson was the father of black children and reveals a great deal about how the United States has defined itself as a nation. It suggests, to use one of our most offensive racist apothegms, that "niggers" were in more places than "the wood pile."

In the discussion of recent revelations that Thomas Jefferson fathered a child or children with his slave concubine Sally Hemings, too much emphasis has been placed on the issue of whether this was a romantic relationship. This focus misses the larger questions at stake. After all, the personal is often political, and in the case of Hemings and Jefferson the political issue raised by their personal relationship is the central one of how we represent our nation and its origins. The fact that first the Founding Fathers and then generations of American historians denied the role that miscegenation played in the creation of New World societies suggests how deeply disturbing the idea of a mixed-race state is to the American conception of a moral nationhood. Fundamental to this notion is a mythic conception of Jefferson. As the historian Joyce Appleby has recently cautioned us, "Presidents serve us as inspirations, and they also serve us as warnings."[47]

Thomas Jefferson occupies a central place in our nation's pantheon of heroes. Author of the Declaration of Independence, third president of the republic, and exemplar of the Enlightenment, Jefferson embodies all the gentlemanly virtues that we are supposed to associate with the Virginia aristocracy. These qualities, in the popular mind, are honor, refinement, and probity — all qualities commonly associated with whiteness. The recent discovery that this American icon was the father of a mixed-race child or children, and the inescapable correlative that he must have had sex with a black woman, has introduced a deep fault line in how the nation thinks about Jefferson, interracial sex, slavery, history, and black women — in brief, how we think about race.

Because the Euro-American understanding of blacks as both physical and intellectual beings developed in slavery, it is here we must begin. Within slavery, black women were not only workers but also objects of sexual exploitation. This facet of slave women's lives has been captured in powerful slave narratives such as *Twelve Years a Slave,* by Solomon Northup, and Harriet Jacobs's *Incidents in the Life of a Slave Girl.* It was also dealt with, albeit obliquely, in popular fiction. More than forty years ago Severn Duvall's brilliant article *"Uncle Tom's Cabin:* The Sinister Side of the Patriarchy" examined this implicit theme of Harriet Beecher Stowe's powerful novel.[48]

As a proper Victorian lady, Stowe only obliquely hinted at what was sexually "going down" on Simon Legree's plantation. Legree, like Jefferson, was involved in a sexual relationship with a slave that, like a homosexual relationship, "dared not speak its name." What I want to argue here is that the metaphor of the closet is not the exclusive possession of homosexuality. The closet also must be understood as a place of hiding for heterosexual acts defined as deviant. Viewed from this perspective, the closet can also function as a place of strength and safety.[49] In the Jeffersonian world there was no place for Jefferson to "come out." Jefferson could not write a narrative of his life comparable to John Gabriel Stedman's *Narrative of a Five Years Expedition against the Revolted Negroes of Surinam* (1796), in which Stedman could proclaim, "I love African Negroes, which I have shown on numberless occasions."[50] Nor could Jefferson leave a diary as scandalous as that of the eighteenth-century Jamaican overseer and planter Thomas Thistlewood, who recorded his numerous sexual encounters with black women in a compulsive fashion.[51]

On the contrary, Jefferson had a secret life that for both political and cultural reasons had to remain "closeted." According to a

Virginia statute of 1622, stiff fines were to be levied against "any Christian [who] shall commit fornication with a negro man or woman."[52] The authors of this law considered sex with a black to be "contrary to nature," in the words of Michel Foucault.[53] Sex between blacks and whites was seen as an abomination that undermined the natural order embodied in slavery. In Thomas Jefferson's Virginia, white men could not openly acknowledge sleeping with black women. To do so would have resulted in legal punishment and, perhaps more damaging in the long run, ostracism. We know that some white men were known to have violated the antimiscegenation statutes and were never prosecuted for doing so.[54] But given his social and political position, Jefferson could not afford to flout either the law or public opinion. Whatever feelings Jefferson may have had for Sally Hemings were circumscribed by a set of cultural and political taboos that made the personal political. There was no institution in Jeffersonian Virginia like the custom of "Surinam marriage," a form of concubinage that John Gabriel Stedman shared with the slave girl Joanna in the eighteenth century:

I must describe this Custom which I am convinced will be highly censured by the Sedate European Matrons — and which is nevertheless common as it is almost necessary to the batchelors who live in the Climate; these Gentlemen all without Exception have a female Slave / mostly a creole / in their keeping who preserves their linnens clean and decent, dresses their Victuals with Skill, carefully attends them / they being most excellent nurses / during the frequent illnesses to which Europeans are exposed in this Country, prevents them from keeping late Hours, knits for them, sows for them &c* — while these Girls who are sometimes Indians sometimes Mulattos and often negroes, naturally pride themselves in living with an European whom they serve with as much tenderness, and to whom they are Generally as faithful as if he were their lawfull

Husband to the great Shame of so many fair Ladies, who break through ties more sacred, and indeed bound with more Solemnity, nor can the above young women be married in any other way, being by their state of Servitude entirely debard from every Christian priviledge and Ceremony, which makes it perfectly lawful on *their* Side, while they hesitate not to pronounce as Harlots, who do not follow them / if they can / in this laudable Example in which they are encouraged as I have said by their nearest Relations and Friends.[55]

Surinam marriage was acceptable in the Dutch colony because Dutch Surinam had far more white men than white women. In Jefferson's Virginia, where the gender ratio was more balanced, there was no such practical imperative for racial mixing and no such matter-of-fact acceptance of interracial sex. In this country, particularly in the seventeenth, eighteenth, and nineteenth centuries, the myth that upper-class white men were averse to black ("trim") sex was part of the racial ideology to which white Americans hypocritically subscribed. I reference white Americans' hypocrisy here because it speaks to the twin processes of denial and attraction that have informed white American attitudes about the subject of interracial sex.

Sally Hemings was not the first black bondswoman to have sex with her master. In fact, recent work on master-slave relations in Albemarle County, the site of Monticello, indicates that sexual encounters between female slaves and their owners were commonplace. A contemporary Virginia judge noted "imprudent (though not uncommon) temporary connections" between young white men and slave girls.[56] Similarly, a minister in Charles City County, Virginia, observed that "the country swarms with mulatto bastards."[57] Nor was this the only county in Virginia where this sort of activity occurred in the eighteenth century. A cleric in Charleston noted that there were "many slaves [who were] only half black, the offspring of those white Sodomites who commit fornication with their black slave women." And Pastor Johann Bolzius expressed a distaste for "amalgamation" when he said that "white men live in sin with negresses and father half black children who walk around in large numbers to the shame of the Christian name."[58] In many parts of the South, sleeping with black women was a rite of passage for both upper- and lower-class white men before, during, and after the age of Jefferson, surviving even into recent history. Writing in the twentieth century about white southern males' sexual mores, both the sociologist John Dollard and the distinguished American historian David B. Davis commented on this practice. Davis, reflecting on his experience in the United States Army during World War II, observed that a number of his southern white peers "boasted that you didn't know what sex could mean unless you had 'laid' a young black 'wench.'"[59]

These men were giving voice to a folkway that dates back to the seventeenth century and was widely practiced in the eighteenth century. Jefferson's own father-in-law had a black mistress, and his friend George Wythe also is alleged to have had one.[60] In brief, interracial sex was normative, if largely unacknowledged, in this aristocratic world we have lost, and the sexual exploitation of black women was a central feature of New World slavery. What makes the Hemings-Jefferson relationship important is Thomas Jefferson's stature as a man of the Enlightenment and a principal architect of the American nation-state. Had Jefferson been a Virginia planter without influence beyond Monticello and the social world of Albemarle County, his sexual relationship with a black bondswoman would have been deemed an unexceptional example of the customs of the colonial South, a bygone era that some would like to think has little relevance in our own time. But Jefferson represents much more, for the Jeffersonian legacy is inextricably linked to the formation of the American republic and, more generally, to the American national character. This fact has made the Hemings-

Jefferson union an extremely vexing issue for some, as it calls into question dearly held contemporary misconceptions about who we are as a nation.

Because Jefferson was and is emblematic of the United States, his apologists see him as blemished if he slept with a black woman. To them, this is the ultimate crime against nature, an unnatural and irrational sexual union. Writing in the twentieth century, Douglass Adair, Virginius Dabney, Dumas Malone, Alf J. Mapp Jr., John C. Miller, Merrill D. Peterson, Willard Sterne Randall, and Douglas Wilson show us that ideas that developed in medieval Christendom still have a hold on our ideas about sexuality and race.[61] Their protestations indicate a need on the part of some white people to deny the possibility that Jefferson transgressed a boundary that his white supporters claim was and is instinctual in white men: an aversion to sleeping with black women. In this racist fantasy, black "coochie" works on white boys like kryptonite. The fact that Jefferson slept with a woman designated as black by what later became the American law of hypodescent, his champions assume, would indicate some personal or national failing that has to be denied.

Earlier generations of Americans contributed to this process of denial in the way they wrote about the colonial South, constructing it as an aberration rather than as emblematic of the nation's attitudes about race and sex. The abolitionists did this in the nineteenth century when they characterized the South as a "brothel."[62] Interracial sex was thus identified as a southern shortcoming, not a national one, and both slavery and miscegenation could be treated as marginal rather than as central to the American story. And when American historians wrote about the past prior to publication of Winthrop Jordan's groundbreaking *White over Black: American Attitudes Toward the Negro, 1550–1812*, race and racial intermixture were not central to their conceptualization of the nation's development. The master narrative of American history was conceptualized instead around the "presidential synthesis," "progressivism," "immigration," "labor," and the "cult of the consensus," to name a few of the paradigms used to give coherence to our nation's past.

For most white Americans, the history of the United States is a history of a white nation. Writing about this problem, the black historian Nathan Huggins observed that "American historians . . . have conspired with the Founding Fathers to create a national history, teleologically bound to the Fathers' ideals rather than reality."[63] The reality of America in 1789, when the Constitution was adopted, was that the land mass that became the United States already held a mixed-race society, not a white one, in which racial intermixture occurred with great frequency. In this context, the importance of the Hemings-Jefferson liaison lies in its symbolic function as a national unifier. It ties black people and other racialized subjects in the United States to the nation's creation, reinforcing what Huggins called "birthright claims."[64] In reality, the nation should recognize Sally and Thomas as its founding parents and abandon the idea that the United States was a white nation from its inception. This will require a jettisoning of the idea that Jefferson, as a white supremacist, was averse to sleeping with a woman designated "black" in the popular imagination and in American law.

For most Americans, black or white, the tale of the Jefferson-Hemings affair is a story of a white man and a woman who was phenotypically Negroid — who, in other words, looked like a Negro. But what is called a "Negro" in America has changed over time. As Benjamin Braude has remarked, "We should not assume the fixity, prominence, or continuity of blackness."[65] Walter White, a novelist and the second secretary of the NAACP, captured the fluidity and paradox of blackness when he wrote, "I am a Negro. My skin is white, my eyes are blue, my hair is blond. The traits of my race are nowhere visible upon me. . . . [But] I am not white. I am one of the two in the color of my skin; I am the other in my spirit and my heart."[66] The statements by Braude and White illuminate the transhistoric problem of defining what is or has been called "black" in America and in Western civilization generally.

The notion that Jefferson found Negroes physically repellent and thus was hostile to sleeping with black people rests on a reading of his *Notes on the State of Virginia*. There Jefferson wrote that the Negroes' "color," "figure," and "hair" were not as attractive as those of whites or Indians, and he derided "the eternal monotony, which reigns in the countenance, that immovable veil of black which covers the emotions." By contrast, he claimed, the superior complexions of Caucasians and Native Americans permitted "the expression of every passion by greater or lesser suffusions of color." Blacks also lacked "flowing hair," emitted "disagreeable body odor," and in general had ungainly bodies.[67] Given Jefferson's publicly expressed antipathy to the black body, he surely would have disagreed with the sentiment that "the blacker the berry the sweeter the juice / I want a real black woman for my special use."[68] How, then, are we to explain Jefferson's thirty-eight-year relationship with Sally Hemings?[69]

In the first place, both historians and the public have to abandon the assumption that Sally Hemings was phenotypically black, that is, visibly Negroid. We do not really know what Hemings looked like. What we do know is that this slave woman was Thomas Jefferson's wife's half-sister and that she came from a black family that had already been transformed by miscegenation. Because both her mother's father and her own were white, Hemings herself was a quadroon and thus probably had features that satisfied "the complex physical (somatic) characteristics" that Caucasians such as Jefferson "defined as [their] norm and ideal."[70] Stated another way, Hemings's features were almost certainly more Caucasoid than Negroid, and in a sense her attractiveness was defined by the absence of black features. She probably had thin lips and a thin nose and hair that was not nappy, if I may speculate here. She probably also was light-skinned. In Jeffersonian Virginia it was possible for a person to be visibly white and yet be a slave because of what later became the law of hypodescent and the fact that one's mother was a slave. Visiting Monticello in 1796, the duc de La Rochefoucauld-Liancourt, for example, claimed to have seen "slaves, who neither in point of color nor features showed the least trace of their original descent."[71]

It would be illuminating and amusing if Hemings could be played in films and on television by someone like Meg Ryan rather than Thandie Newton. This casting option would return us to the conventions of an earlier generation of films such as *Lost Boundaries* (1949), *Imitation of Life* (1934 and 1956), and *Pinky* (1949), in which the blackness of some of the characters is depicted as genotype, not phenotype, by which I mean that black physiognomy was not discernible.[72] In *Lost Boundaries*, for example, the Carter family is white in appearance except for the son, who could be either a mulatto or a Negroid Latino and is darker than the rest of the family. In the 1934 version of *Imitation of Life*, the part of the octoroon daughter was played by the actress Fredi Washington. Although Washington was black, most viewers of the movie thought she was white, and only the most discerning of eyes would have read her as a person of Negro ancestry. When *Imitation of Life* was remade in 1956, the role was given to a white actress, Susan Kohner. In both versions of the film the octoroon daughter passes as white until her phenotypically — which is to say, visibly — black mother dies. What makes *Lost Boundaries*, *Imitation of Life*, and *Pinky* interesting is that in none of these films is race "a fixed external reality recognizably embodied and encoded in skin color."[73] In both versions of *Imitation of Life*, although the mother has a black physiognomy, the child "reads" visually as white. Both Louise Beavers and Juanita Moore, in cinematically giving birth to phenotypically white children, confound the conundrum "Why is it a white woman can give birth to a black child, but a black woman can never give birth to a white child?"[74] Having more movies that use the racial mode of analysis found in *Lost Boundaries, Imitation of Life,* and *Pinky* would healthily complicate the belief that skin color is always a signifier of race. More importantly, it would help eliminate the misconception that Thomas Jefferson, as a phenotypic racist, would never have taken Sally Hemings as his mistress.

Although it is important to understand that physically Hemings would not have fit preconceived notions of phenotypical blackness, we are still faced with the fact that legally and culturally she was identified as black. Jefferson's concubine was, in short, a member of a race that Jefferson is on record as regarding as "inferior to the whites in the endowments both of body and mind."[75] How do we deal with this paradox?

Here we should note the existence in the colonial period of the idea that the taint of blackness would be removed from the black racialized subject by three to five generations of interracial sex. In 1783 Henry Laurens, an antislavery merchant and patriot, wrote to William Drayton that "by perseverance the black may be blanched and the stamp of Providence effectually effaced."[76] Laurens was part of a conversation about blacks' color that at various moments also included Edward Long and Thomas Jefferson. Writing in his *History of Jamaica,* Long observed, "The descendants of the Negroe blood, entitled to all the rights and liberties of white subjects, in the full extent, are such, who are above three steps removed in lineal digression from the Negroe *venter* exclusive; that is to say, real *quinterons,* for all below this degree are reputed by law *Mulattos.*"[77] Jefferson was aware of this "classificatory calculus" when he replied to a query in 1815 from Francis C. Gray, who asked him, "At what point does a black man become white?" Jefferson's answer was a variant of Long's. "You asked me in conversation, what constituted a mulatto by our law.... Our canon considers two crosses with the pure white, and a third with any degree of mixture, however small, as clearing the issue of Negro blood."[78] Any children Hemings and Jefferson produced were three or more degrees removed from blackness. In fact, if they had lived in eighteenth-century Jamaica, they would have been legally white.[79]

The preceding quotation has to be juxtaposed with another Jeffersonian discussion of mixed-race children, however. In a letter written in 1814 to his friend Edward Coles, Jefferson said the following about racial mixing: "The amalgamation of whites with blacks produces a degradation to which no lover of his country, no lover of excellence in the human character can innocently consent."[80] While some will read these statements as indicating that Jefferson was a man of contradictions, I do not. The first comment is legal; the other is cultural and biological. Something else can also be discerned in Jefferson's and Long's observations, namely, the historical power of white people to say who is and who is not white. This is why Jefferson could sleep with Hemings without experiencing cognitive dissonance, I would argue. Intimately acquainted with the history of the Hemings family, Jefferson could see the physical transformation from black to white within the Hemings clan across generations. Possibly he did not see in Sally and her affines the physical or mental degeneration that was supposed to characterize someone of mixed racial descent. Perhaps he persuaded himself that in some fundamental way, as well as in her physical appearance, she was not black and that in any possible offspring of theirs the stain of blackness would be even further bleached. Or perhaps, in the end, his attraction to Hemings owed less to philosophical hairsplitting than to simple sexual desire.

In their treatment of Jefferson, historians of the pre-DNA era focused too much on his writings, arguing that he could not possibly have slept with Hemings because of his published views on black people. What they ignored was that repression often coexists with desire. Writing in 1810, the African Methodist minister and colonizationist Daniel Coker, commenting on "amalgamation," observed that "some of the high rank, and who profess abhorrence to such connections, have been the first in the transgression."[81] As the sociologist John Dollard wrote many years ago, "Sexual behavior is almost always more complex than it appears, and deep taboos and anxieties are in most cases associated with it; but certainly the factor of straight sexual desire must play a role."[82] People's sexual practices are unruly, as Winthrop Jordan understood when he wrote that "the sexual desire of human beings has always, in the long run, overridden even the strongest sense of difference between two groups of human beings."[83] It also is possible for white men and black women to love each other, a point often forgotten in our cynical and highly politicized readings of the past.

We can better understand Jefferson's relationship with Hemings if we place it in the context of his ideas about intermarriage with Native Americans. On 18 February 1803, in a letter to Benjamin Hawkins, Jefferson predicted a dismal future for Native Americans if they were not absorbed into white society. "In truth, the ultimate point of rest & happiness for them is to let our settlements and theirs meet and blend together, to intermix and become one people. Incorporating themselves with us as citizens of the U.S., this is what the natural progress of things will of course bring on, and it will be better to promote than retard it. Surely it will be better for them to be identified with us."[84] Jefferson could champion intermarriage with Native Americans because they were somatically closer to whites than were blacks. Also, he "did not hate Indians. Instead, he hated their degraded condition," Peter Onuf has written.[85] Marriage with Native Americans was possible because they possessed the potential to become white that blacks lacked. As the anthropologist Anthony F. C. Wallace has noted, "Indians could be regarded as inherently the equals of whites and yet as culturally inferior, child like, in their savage state."[86] Jefferson was not alone in thinking that intermarriage with Native Americans was a good thing for the future of Indians and the United States. Writing sixty-five years earlier, William Byrd of Westover, in his

Histories of the Dividing Line betwixt Virginia and North Carolina, had advanced a similar line of argument. Byrd also thought that the amalgamation of white and red would be easy "if a Moor may be washed white in three generations"; because Moors were black, a comparable act of racial transformation could be accomplished more quickly with Indians.[87] According to Byrd, because Indians were lighter complexioned, "their copper-coloured Complexion would admit of blanching, if not in the first, at farthest in the Second Generation."[88]

According to Byrd's logic, Indians were more acceptable bed partners for whites for two reasons. First, it took only two crossings (generations) for Indians to become lighter complexioned, whereas it required at least three crossings for blacks to satisfy the white somatic norm, black being a darker color than red. Second, embedded in both Byrd's and Jefferson's advocacy of red and white intermarriage was the assumption that Indians were culturally and physically assimilable. This process was facilitated by the fact that the Native Americans were dying out and thus posed no threat to the future of white supremacy in Virginia. In brief, sex and intermarriage with Native Americans did not change either whites' color or their temperament. This was not the case with black slaves, whose Africanness most Americans considered to be ineradicable and thus a danger to the nation. In addition, blacks' numbers were increasing in Virginia, posing a threat to social and racial stability.[89]

Neither Byrd nor Jefferson was being racially progressive in suggesting that whites and Native Americans intermarry. Amalgamation of red and white was a strategy to preserve whiteness, for black, red, and white were defined by their relationship to intermixture, and within this chiaroscuro whites were always pure.

Jefferson's belief in the whiteness of America can be seen in his efforts to free what Barbara J. Fields, writing in another context, has called a "fractional pariah."[90] The object of Jefferson's concern was an indentured servant named Samuel Howell, who in 1769, in what came to be known as the case of *Howell v. Netherland,* asked Jefferson to free him from indentured servitude.[91] Jefferson's efforts to emancipate Howell suggest that color played some part in the Sage of Monticello's endeavors to liberate the indentured servant. Howell's family, like those of Sally Hemings and Daniel Coker, the first bishop of the African Methodist Episcopal Church, was a product of America's heterosexual closet.[92] Howell's mother and grandmother were illegitimate and had been relegated to indentured servitude. "Both," according to Gary Nash, "had been trapped by laws passed in 1705 and 1723 to punish racial mixing. The 1705 law sentenced the offspring of a white woman and a black or mulatto man to thirty-one years of labor, and the 1723 statute held that any child born of such a white woman, even if the father was white, would be held in servitude for thirty-one years if the mother herself was also in servitude."[93] The issue for Jefferson in this case, I would argue, was both Howell's condition of servitude and his color. Jefferson thought that Howell, being white and "entirely blameless for [his] degraded condition," should not be held in servitude. Jefferson opposed the claims of Howell's master, a man named Netherland, on the grounds that his interpretation of the laws of 1705 and 1723 was too expansive. Netherland's reading of the law, said Jefferson, "would make servants of the children of white servants or apprentices, which nobody will say is right."[94] The legal historian Paul Finkelman makes an important point when he notes, in discussing the case of *Howell v. Netherland,* Jefferson's argument that "under law of nature . . . we are all born free."[95] But whom did Jefferson mean by "we"?

Howell's white appearance, like that of Jefferson's children with Hemings, I think persuaded the future third president that Howell and his slave progeny were white and thus European. It may be that for Jefferson the racial identity of the Hemingses and of Howell had been transformed by either sex or love and thus they could be included in his "we." Jefferson may have followed the example of Jamaica, where, according to Edward Long, "the children of a white and Quarteroon [were] called English" and thus were white, and not freaks of nature.[96]

Howell's whiteness enabled him to sue in court for his freedom, albeit unsuccessfully. Whiteness also facilitated the efforts of Jefferson and Hemings' children — Beverly, Eston, and Harriet — to run away from their controversial racial past. Their presence in white society did not pose a challenge to America's white racial identity. Passing, as Philip Roth, in his wonderful novel *The Human Stain,* has recently reminded us, is as American as apple pie. Commenting on his protagonist, Coleman Silk, Roth makes it clear that blacks have no monopoly on passing:

He wants to separate himself from the predicament into which he was born. Not the first person to want to do that. You needn't be Jewish to like Levi's rye bread, they used to say. Many people in America particularly have had the opportunity to abandon origins they didn't want to bother with; that they felt imprisoned by, that they felt compromised by, that they felt ashamed of, that they felt were encumbrances of one kind or another. And who is to say that people have no right to throw off skins if they can throw them off — in pursuit of happiness; especially in a country where it was very possible to disappear. People disappear in America. So he has a background which is right in the American grain, Coleman Silk.[97]

Beverly, Eston, and Harriet, as the children of the third president of the United States, also had a background "in the American grain." They, like many other "fractional pariahs," exercised the defining freedom of American racial culture and passed. In a society in which so many fair-skinned black people have exercised this option, why should we be surprised that Jefferson and Hemings's progeny decided not to be what W. E. B. Du Bois once referred to as a "problem," that is, black.[98] They passed because being Caucasian was the badge of privilege in early national America. Passing enabled the Hemings children to escape what Frantz Fanon has called "the pit of nigger hood."[99]

In the pre–Civil War United States the "pit of nigger hood" was the place assigned to what Hayden White called "arrested humanity."[100] It was a site that De Tocqueville described as depriving "the descendants of the Africans of almost all the privileges of humanity."[101] In the early republic, blacks were regarded as creatures of nature whose lives were governed by appetite rather than by reason. Civilized people — whites — "because of science, industry, Christianity, and racial excellence," had progressed beyond the primal state.[102] I should note here that the escape of the Jefferson-Hemings progeny from this perceived pit or primal state was not without its painful consequences. "Passing," as the legal scholar Patricia Williams has written, "is the practice of orphaning oneself."[103] In leaving behind the "pit of nigger hood," Eston, Beverly, and Harriet had to deny who they were.

What passing meant in the antebellum United States was the denial of the possibility of mixed race. One was either black or white in Jefferson's time and well afterward. But to stop our reading here is to miss a greater complication in our nation's racial history. Americans' insistence on seeing Jefferson and Hemings's production of nonwhite, nonblack children as an interpersonal, individual act bleaches out our past and reaffirms the hegemony of whiteness. Paradoxically, on the structural-political level, that very act of producing nonwhite, nonblack children served to undermine that hegemony. Only on the unconscious, public, and collective levels can these acts of miscegenation constitute contestation. What the history of passing in the Hemings family indicates is the "failure of 'race' to impose stable definitions of identity, or to manifest itself in reliable, permanent and or visible manner."[104] Interracial sex simultaneously liberated Hemings and Jefferson's children and subverted the nation's racial boundaries.

Whether we call it a mode of production or slavery, black bondage was a labor system easily derailed by the foibles of both the master and the slaves. In brief, to quote Henry Wiencek, "human impulse was the great enemy of the slave system."[105] Gilberto Freyre understood this when he wrote about Brazilian slavery, observing that "there is no slavery without sexual depravity."[106] Interracial sex brought into question the racial premise of slavery that only black people were slaves. The production of generations of "fractional pariahs" created over time a population that was white in appearance. These people were proof that the claim of white racists that whites were repelled by sex with blacks or people of Negro ancestry was false. Jefferson occupies a central place in this narrative.

Central to the denial of the Jefferson-Hemings affair has been an effort to deflect attention from the likelihood that Jefferson was highly sexed.[107] Before Jefferson's marriage, he tried to seduce another man's wife. After his wife's death, Jefferson had a brief affair with a married woman in Paris. His wife, Martha Wayles, bore six children in ten years, and some historians have suggested that her youthful demise was caused by these pregnancies. To put it less delicately, it is possible that the Sage of Monticello "rogered" his wife to death.[108] This apparent degree of sexual appetite is at odds with the popular image of a man who has been approvingly described not only as thinking that passion had to be controlled "by the exercise of reason" but also as possessing "feminine temperament."[109] To describe Jefferson as a man of restrained sexuality seems to suggest that once he was widowed at the age of forty-one, he lost his sex drive and became passionless. It also presupposes, as the Puritans did, that character is based on the refusal of desire. To preserve Jefferson's reputation, his defenders have created in the popular mind the image of a Founding Father with the heroic capacity for self-denial of an early Christian desert father. But to construct Jefferson in those terms is to entertain one of the major fantasies of Western, and specifically Anglo-Saxon, whiteness since the Age of Discovery and the Enlightenment: the illusion of self-control over the venereal. But as the philosopher Arnold Davidson has written, "Chastity and virginity are moral categories denoting a relation between the will and the flesh; they are not categories of sexuality."[110] In attempting to place Jefferson's sexuality in a category with which they felt comfortable, his partisans, both pre- and post-DNA, fell victim to what the French historian of science Georges Canguilhem has called the "virtue of the precursors." Arnold Davidson says of this fallacy that "we perpetually look for precursors to our categories of sexuality in essentially different domains, producing anachronisms at best and unintelligibility at worst."[111] The pre- and post-DNA deniers did not place the Jefferson-Hemings affair in the long sweep of white men's encounters with women in Africa, Asia, and the New World but instead imposed a Victorian sexual sensibility on a context in which it did not belong. In particular, they were, and are, silent about the troubled sexual history of blacks and Euro-Americans in North America.

As Winthrop Jordan and other historians have noted, the English in particular were disturbed by what they imagined to be black sexual practice and defined themselves sexually in opposition to blackness. Whiteness came to embody self-control, and black, its opposite. Deeply embedded in this belief was an anxiety about sexual potency. Although Jefferson was sexually potent, he directly expressed his anxiety on this point in his writings about black people. I am referring here to the observation that "they are more ardent after their females, but love seems with them to be more eager desire, than a tender delicate sentiment and sensation."[112] In this passage Jefferson articulates the Euro-American mythology that Caucasian sex was "vanilla," that is, unsullied by either passion or imagination. For whites of Jefferson's class and time, sex was construed as a duty and a burden, the principal aim of which was propagation of children. In the Jeffersonian world, according to Brenda Stevenson, "white people married and blacks copulated."[113] It is this context that frames Jefferson's observations about the "ardent" nature of black sex. How did Jefferson know what black sex was like? Maybe he had engaged in fieldwork and stopped being a philosophical and conjectural historian. I say this because the description of black sex as "ardent" can be read as an example of a projection fantasy, an observation in which Jefferson, although ostensibly speaking about blacks, was really talking about himself.

Jefferson's characterization of black sexuality as ardent was consonant with a white Western perception of black sex as animalistic. This notion had been around since the days of the Roman Empire, when black people, *Aethiopes,* were stereotyped as hypersexual. The birth of Christianity did nothing to efface this thinking. As the classical historian Lloyd A. Thompson has written, "Christian linkage of blackness with sin favored this association of *Aethiopes* with sexuality, inducing some people to see blacks as dark and mysterious sources of forbidden (and so heightened) sexual pleasure."[114] In a thirteenth-century lecture on the subject of whether women "produce seed," Albertus Magnus told students in Cologne that "such seed is found more in black women than white women — more in black women who engage in sex more than all women. For black women are hotter — and most of all dusky women — who are the sweetest to have sex with, as lechers say — and because the mouth of their vulva is temperate and gently embraces the penis."[115] As both Sander Gilman and Winthrop Jordan have argued, ideas about black sex being animal-like were still alive and thriving in the sixteenth and seventeenth centuries, when Europeans came to think that African women copulated with apes and African men were described as having "large Propogaters."[116] The myth of the "macrophallic" black male became an urtext of Western male "scrotum sociology." The counterpart to this fantasy about black male genitalia was a comparable marking of the black vagina as the site of copulative bliss.

To white people, black sex seemed exotic not only because of their fantasies about black genitalia but also because of black people's presumed sexual intercourse with animals. Sexual congress with animals (which, among other things, implies the nonprocreative act of sodomy) marked black sex "as inherently different and corrupt, giving rise to representations of black sexuality as bestial. Blacks were animals because they had sex with animals."[117] Edward Long called sexual congress between a black woman and a white man a "goatish embrace."[118] The representation of interracial sex as animalistic suggests something unnatural, or, in Michel Foucault's words, "against the law."[119] Interracial sex, whether engaged in by Jefferson or by any other white male, was marked as a transgression against whiteness. It was a dual form of racial treason, both biological and rational, the latter indicating a loss of control. Although there is no evidence that African women slept with apes or that black male genitalia were or are larger than those of Euro-American males, variations on these fantasies informed Jefferson's discussion of black sexuality. For Jefferson and other white Americans, blackness was more than a question of color; it was also an issue of "underdevelopment," the rational faculties of Negroes being overridden by their physical appetites.[120]

From the outset, the figure of Sally Hemings herself was put squarely into this hypersexualized context by her detractors. James Callender, in the first published allegations of the affair, portrayed her as "romping with half a dozen black fellows." Allegedly her libidinousness was unrestrained and indiscriminate. According to Callender, Hemings had "fifteen or thirty gallants of all colours" and was a "slut common as the pavement." Callender's fantasy about Hemings was shared by Thomas Gibbons, a Georgia Federalist, who wrote in a letter of 20 December 1802 that "she is the most abandoned prostitute of her color — Pampered into a lascivious course of life, with the benefits of a French Education, she is more lecherous than other beasts of the Monticellan Mountain."[121] Reading these descriptions of Hemings, one might conclude that she was Monticello's version of Valeria Messalina, the supposedly nymphomaniacal wife of the Roman emperor Claudius.[122]

It is entirely possible that in his sex life with Hemings, Jefferson found a sexual excitement that was absent in his marriage with Martha. Given the sexual mythology that had developed around the black female body since ancient times and that in the New World in the seventeenth and eighteenth centuries had come to signify a corporal difference between white and black women, Jefferson may have found Hemings to be sexually exciting simply because he expected that she, as a black woman, would be.

Added to the stimulus of racially transgressive sex was the fact that the relationship crossed class lines as well. We can gain insight into this aspect of the Hemings-Jefferson liaison by considering the romance and marriage of Hannah Cullwick and Arthur Munby. Although it dates from well after the death of Jefferson, their story bears a close resemblance in several crucial respects to that of Jefferson and Hemings.[123] Cullwick, a maid, and Munby, an upper-class British barrister and *litterateur,* were secret lovers for eighteen years and married for thirty-six. What we know about this couple comes from the diaries left by Cullwick and from Munby's will. Munby liked "butch" working-class women. He was, as Liz Stanley points out, obsessed with "lower class women who were truly working women, whether in the coal pits of Wigan or the digging roads of London."[124] Munby's sexual tastes were paralleled by Jefferson's preference for "enslaved sexuality."[125] As the psychoanalytical critic Helen Moglen has written, "Desire is performed within history at the intersection of gender, race, sexuality and class."[126] The Jefferson-Hemings relationship encompassed all of these variables.

Both Munby's and Jefferson's obsessions with women who were their social inferiors suggest the *idée fixe* of male homosexuals of the Victorian and Edwardian eras who were obsessed with the vitality of lower-class men. This preoccupation is examined sympathetically in E. M. Forster's novel *Maurice,* and it is the subtext of D. H. Lawrence's *Lady Chatterley's Lover,* where the female protagonist's sexuality is brought to maturity by her working-class gardener. Cullwick and Munby seem to have inhabited the netherworld of "nonvanilla" sex, drawn to sexual practices outside the range of supposedly heteronormative sexuality. "For years up until their marriage Hannah wore a padlock and a chain around her neck, to which only Munby had the key." She also called him "Massa," blackened her face, and from time to time "licked his boots" and "washed his feet."[127] These interactions, with their overtones of slavery, today would be labeled kinky by the prosaic and depraved by the morally self-righteous. But in the Victorian world they were part of a vast underground in which both the bourgeoisie and the aristocracy participated.[128]

American historians can learn much about sexual relationships between upper-class men and lower-class women by studying the Munby-Cullwick affair. It illuminates some of the problems attendant upon studying Jefferson and making claims that recent evidence has shown to be questionable. Horror of horrors, what if Thomas Jefferson, one of the fathers of our country, was bored by women of his own race and class and took a black woman slave to bed? Sex is a complex, often irrational impulse, and just why some people find other people attractive remains elusive. Writing about this issue, Paul Robinson observed, "Sex . . . is a rudely physical, indeed animal, need for the pleasure we get doing particular things with particular parts of our bodies. This is true for intellectuals as it is anyone else. Sex is an often humbling experience for intellectuals precisely because it reminds them, so unconditionally, of the extent to which they are pure *geist*."[129] In the case of Sally Hemings and Thomas Jefferson, all we know for sure is that they engaged in sex and produced a child or children. Jefferson's feelings about the relationship and about Hemings herself remain a mystery.

The story is equally opaque, if not more so, as seen from Hemings's perspective. What we know about slavery and the sexual exploitation of black women under that system makes it easy to assume that the relationship was purely an instance of a powerful white man taking advantage of a powerless black woman. Yet this may not have been the case. When the Hemings-Jefferson relationship is understood as combining desire on his part with a strategy for survival on hers, it is possible to see that both parties may have had something to gain from the relationship. This line of argument requires that we rethink the problem of interracial sex in slavery and abandon the idea that all sexual encounters between white men and black women were rapes.[130]

To construct all sexual encounters between white masters and female black slaves as rape is to misread the complexity of human sexuality. As Jeffrey Weeks has cautioned us, "The various definitions of what we call only for convenience the 'sexual' vary enormously through time and across cultures and subcultures. Yet we apparently need to believe that as things are so they have always been, rooted in our essential natures (the 'truth of our being')."[131] This admonition is very important when we use the word *rape*. It is ahistorical to assume that what we would call rape today was defined as rape in the past. Sharon Block has cautioned against making this error: "Rape may have been a physically abusive act, but violence alone did not make a sexual act rape. The violence was the proof of the lack of control, not the cause of the attack. For us, sex might be categorized as violent when it degrades or destroys or damages. For early Americans, the passions of sex were already violent."[132]

For most slave women, the social practice of sexual violence meant that they were frequently the objects of their masters' lust. But to see female slaves solely as sexual victims is to deprive them of sexual agency and ignores the fact that the penis was not the only body part with agency.[133] The vagina is also a historical agent, and it was only in the late eighteenth and nineteenth centuries, in the "Cult of True Womanhood," that women came to be seen as sexually passive.[134] This ideology of virtue, originally the cultural property of middle-class white women, was extended to black women in the abolitionist critique of slavery during the antebellum period of American history. In the depiction of the South as a site of sexual license, black women were portrayed as the victims of both white and black male lasciviousness.

It would be a mistake to assume from what I have written so far that I think there was no such thing as rape in slavery. There certainly was sexual violence, but not all relationships involving black women and white men were coercive. I therefore take exception to such generalizing sentiments as this: "What does sexuality designate when rape is a normative mode of its deployment? How can rape be differentiated from sexuality when 'consent' is intelligible only as submission?"[135] This statement strips the historical actor, in this case Hemings, of autonomy. It makes her a cipher, and not an agent in a relationship that lasted thirty-eight years.

Kathleen Brown provides a way of understanding some mixed-race affairs when she writes, "The truth of many interracial relationships may lie somewhere between consent and exploitation, with individuals making choices in a context warped and circumscribed by slavery."[136] Brown's observation receives support in the work of Hillary Beckles, a historian of female slavery in the West Indies. Beckles suggests to students of black bondage that "care should be taken not to deny the existence of a considerable degree of socio-sexual autonomy achieved by some enslaved women with respect to particular relationships."[137] This point is also made by Rosalind Mitchison and Leah Leneman when they write that "conception, within or without wedlock, is not parthenogenetic. . . . Unless we are to see the entire male sex as invariably set on seduction we must enquire into the motives and deliberations of both parents."[138] This was true in all slave systems where there were sexual encounters between men and women, either of the same or of different races.

The slave woman Harriet Jacobs, for example, simultaneously resisted and accommodated herself to the sexual approaches of white men. In her autobiographical *Incidents in the Life of a Slave Girl,* Jacobs describes how, although she spurned the sleazy importunings of "Dr. Flint," she was seduced by the overtures of "Mr. Sands." Jacobs takes responsibility for her affair with Sands, observing in her memoir, "I know I did wrong. No one can feel it more sensibly than I do. The painful and humiliating memory will haunt me to my dying day."[139] Jacobs does not present herself as a passive victim of white male lust: "I will not try to screen myself behind the plea of compulsion from a master; for it was not so. Neither can I plead ignorance or thoughtlessness. . . . I knew what I did, and I did it with deliberate calculation." What motivated Jacobs to sleep with Sands was a complex of motives that she variously describes as "revenge," "calculations of self interest," and "gratitude for kindness."[140] She also was pursuing a strategy that she thought would protect her children: "Of a man who was not my master I could ask to have my children well supported; and in this case I felt confident I should obtain the boon. I also felt sure they would be made free."[141]

Just as Jacobs thus exercised the full range of her sexual agency as a female slave, Sally Hemings may have done the same with Thomas Jefferson. Although Hemings ultimately had no power to refuse sex with Jefferson, to some extent she may have taken advantage of Jefferson's apparent eagerness to engage in a long-term liaison with her. Taking this view, we might conjecture that Sally Hemings — and the other women in her immediate family — engaged in a form of sexual social mobility. As Stephanie Camp has written, "For two generations before [Sally,] black women in her family had engaged in sexual relations with powerful white men."[142] Mary Hemings, Sally's sister, was the paramour of the merchant Thomas Bell sometime in the 1780s and bore him two children.[143] Was this family of fair-skinned black women deliberately producing children of light enough complexion to pass "as a collective enterprise staged within the context of intergenerational familial relations"?[144] To answer this question, we must first consider another, even more fundamental issue: Did Sally and her family think of themselves as black? Or did they, like the fair-skinned *gens de colour* of Haiti, consider themselves not to be black or Negro at all?

Historians, filmmakers, and most black and white Americans have assumed in their discussions and representations of the Jefferson-Hemings affair that members of the Hemings family identified themselves as black. This assumption, however, is as unwarranted as the notion that they all had dark skin, broad lips, a broad nose, and nappy hair. It rests on an overdetermined racial reading of slavery that fails to take into account the role color played in the creation of black society during and after slavery. As the anthropologist Suzanna Sawyer has noted, "Problems of representation arise in assuming that subaltern subjects share a unified subject position because they have been silenced by history"; she warns that "subaltern subjects do not represent an already preconstituted cohesive entity, a coherent class."[145] In other words, it is time for a more nuanced look at black culture, one that allows for variations in perspectives and attitudes among black Americans both inside and outside the context of slavery. What we know about the black female experience in American Negro slavery should not lead us to conclude that black women were united in some single, shared consciousness based on their subjectivity. Not all women defined as black identified or perceived themselves as black.

Indeed, the experience of the Hemings women raises important questions about the "linear collective identity model," which has functioned as the major paradigm for the study of American Negro slavery for almost forty years.[146] The use of the phrase *slave community* has obscured as much as it has revealed. Historians of American Negro slavery have equated cultural expression with racial, group, and social identity. In the work of historians such as John Blassingame, Eugene D. Genovese, Herbert Gutman, Lawrence W. Levine, George Rawick, and Sterling Stuckey, culture operates like Linus's blanket, being both reassuring and so expansive that it covers everything.[147] The fact that slaves sang spirituals, told folk tales, believed in "hants," and danced does not mean that these cultural practices had a uniform meaning that created a collective identity that we can label as "slave culture." It is possible and indeed probable that the web of cultural practice produced in the slave quarters had a diverse impact on slaves because they were divided along lines of gender, color, work, age, sexual preference, and religious affiliation.

In their discussion of the oppressed, progressive scholars have tended to see resistance everywhere in slavery and, moreover, to idealize their subjects. The late Herbert Aptheker gave voice to this sentiment when he wrote that "the basic integrity of the masses will be untouched."[148] This, I would suggest, is historical fantasy. It both presumes that there was a unified consciousness among the subaltern and fails to account for the fact that some people within the oppressed benefited from oppression. This was certainly true within the "plantation complex," where some house servants who received preferential treatment thought they were superior to field hands. In addition, throughout the history of the peculiar institution there have been slaves who betrayed their fellow slaves during escapes and slave revolts.[149] My point here is that there was no transhistoric "slave identity"; on the contrary, there was enormous variation in how people defined themselves during slavery. If the self is constructed, there cannot have been an essentialized slave identity. "The creation of identity is a constant negotiation of varying impressions . . . the creation of identity is by no means one's passive reaction to a specific environment," Mieko Nishida has written.[150]

All of the preceding has to be kept in mind when considering women like Sally Hemings and others living in slavery, postslavery emancipation, or racially stratified colonial societies where color is a mark of privilege. Sally Hemings was a slave, but this did not mean that her sense of self derived solely from bondage or from the racial category to which she legally belonged; "identity," according to Nishida, "often differs from a category imposed on the individual by the larger society."[151]

As we have seen, whiteness as a racial ascription in the history of the United States has been more than a racial signifier: it also is a marker with a host of other meanings, including civilization. Opposed to that has been the negative reading of blackness in Euro-American culture and history as uncivilized, expressed in Jefferson's observation, quoted previously, that blacks were "inferior to the whites in the endowments both of body and mind."[152] This construction of blackness as the negative reference point of whiteness cannot have escaped the women of the Hemings family, Sally Hemings included. The Hemings women, like the eighteenth-century Barbadian slave woman Old Doll, two of her daughters (Dolly and Jenny), and Doll's half-sister Mary Ann, the historian Hillary McD. Beckles has written, "aspired to socio-sexual relations with free men, particularly whites, and considered success in this as symbolic of achievement and status."[153]

Beckles further illuminates this strategy when he writes, "By systematic 'whitening' of children through conscious selection of mates, these women sought to diminish the threat of unfreedom. Mary Ann, for example, herself a mulatto, had four children by Thomas Saer, a white man, which were described by Wood [the plantation manager] to be "as white as himself." As the socioeconomic position of this family improved, Beckles writes, "its members also became increasingly whiter as a result of miscegenation." The estate manager Sampson Wood reported that the younger females of the family "either have or had white husbands, that is, men who keep them." Mary Thomas, the daughter of Mary Ann, for example, "had a long standing sexual relation with the white bookkeeper by whom she had a son." Other women in the family also had white partners. What is interesting about this group of women, as Beckles observes, is that "the records do not suggest that they had any intimate relations with slave men, but such relations seem unlikely given the women's perceptions of elitism, authority, and self esteem."[154]

If we broaden our perspective, a similar pattern of "sleeping white" can also be seen in the Dutch colony of South Africa. In that colony, mixed-race slave women, according to Robert C. H. Shell, cohabited with and married white men in order that "the next generation might fare better."[155] A classic example is the case of Manda Gratia, who in 1714 married a wealthy Dutch burgher named Guilliam Frisnet. This marriage enabled Manda "to free nearly all of her previous offspring. One freed mulatto son promptly joined the Dutch East India Company and set sail for the East Indies, the first slave emigrant from the colony."[156]

We can see this strategy even more clearly in societies where there were large Amerindian populations and few white women. The Brazilian chronicler Capistrano de Abreu, for example, observed that "on the part of the Indian women miscegenation is to be explained by the ambition to bear sons belonging to the superior race according to the ideas current among them, it was only parentage on the paternal side that counted."[157] The strategy also carried over into societies where slaves had been emancipated, as can be seen in the testimony of Reyita, a twentieth-century black Cuban woman who married a white Cuban man to ensure her children a better future.

> I didn't want a black husband, not out of contempt for my race, but because black men had no possibilities of getting ahead and the certainty of facing a lot of discrimination.... This is what I didn't want for the children I was going to have. That's why I asked my *Virgencita* for a white husband. I wouldn't have been able to put up with seeing my children humiliated, harassed, mistreated, and much less living a life of vice. That's why I married a white man.[158]

As Trevor Burnard has written, "Interracial relations gave some black women an entree into the white world and some space for themselves within the all encompassing structures of white male dominance."[159] They also offered black American women a chance to improve their children's status within their own race, because while color was a point of tension between black and white, it was also a site of friction between black and black. Explorations of internal color prejudice within black America have not been the subject of insightful historical analysis. This is unfortunate because color has historically constituted one of the major points of division and contention within black America. The most insightful work on this subject has been done by novelists such as Charles W. Chesnutt, Nella Larsen, Wallace Thurman, and most recently Philip Roth.[160] Examination of this fact of black life sheds light on power, gender, identity, sexuality, and partner choice and suggests yet another reason why the Hemings women slept with white men.

If we consider Jefferson's attentions to be advantageous, Sally Hemings's situation is certainly a perfect illustration of sociologist Oliver Cox's dictum that "the lighter the complexion, the greater the economic and social opportunities."[161] Both their color and their relationship to the Jefferson family gave the Hemings women opportunities that most slaves never experienced. While there undoubtedly were light-skinned slaves in the "plantation complex" whose color did not alter their status, on Jefferson's plantation light-skinned bondspeople performed less onerous tasks and were never hired out. Sally even accompanied Jefferson and his family to France, where she lived as a temporarily free woman in close proximity to the highest circles of white European cultural and diplomatic society.[162] I would suggest that Sally Hemings, having grown up at Monticello as the child of house servants and having then left the plantation altogether as part of Jefferson's entourage, was well aware of the prerogatives of fair skin. This consciousness may have been passed on to her progeny. As we have seen, three of her children took advantage of their family's special relationship to the Jeffersons by passing out of the "race."

In terms of the early, widespread prevalence of miscegenation, the United States clearly has much in common with other multiracial societies. The crucial difference lies in how other societies have accepted miscegenation as a vital factor in their historical development. In Brazil, Cuba, and Mexico, for example, sex between men of the master race and women of the Indian and Negro castes was and is an accepted part of those countries' histories. As early as 1844 the German naturalist Friedrich Philip Von Martius commented on a Brazilian nation inhabited by three races as follows: "Anyone who would endeavor to write a history of Brazil, a country so full of promise, should never lose sight of which elements vie for the development of its people. These people, however, are the result of a convergence of three races and are diverse in the extreme."[163] Admittedly, Von Martius's point of view did not go unchallenged, and throughout the nineteenth century and into the twentieth there was a debate among Brazilian historians and intellectuals about the role of race mixture in their nation's development.[164] Ultimately, however, the people who thought that miscegenation was a good thing won the debate in Brazil. The publication in 1933 of Gilberto Freyre's flawed masterpiece *The Masters and the Slaves* ushered in a reevaluation of Brazil's history in which the idea that interracial sex was pathological was abandoned. "By placing miscegenation within the broader context of evolutionary social and economic forces," A. J. R. Russell-Wood wrote, "[Freyre] was able to demonstrate that indeed miscegenation had been a positive factor."[165] In Freyre's book, race is a contingent, not an essential, category. The importance and relevance here lie in Freyre's argument that sex between black women and white men was not pathological or degenerate. As Freyre wrote, "Would not the mixing, on the contrary, have brought to the Brazilian a new beauty . . . Would not the mixing have given to the Brazilian a special resistance to the climate in certain respect . . ."[166] In Freyre's work, interracial sex was progressive and not shameful, because it bred the "new man of Brazil."[167] Interracial sex improved both black and white physiognomy and the culture of the nation. Moreover, Freyre understood that sex was a central component of slavery, commenting that "the most productive feature of slave property is the generative belly."[168]

Miscegenation also served another function in Brazilian slavery. It was not only a site of physical fusion but also a bridge between black and white cultures. As Freyre noted, "A widely practiced miscegenation tended to modify the enormous social distance that otherwise would have been preserved between big house and slave hut."[169] This stands in sharp contrast to U. B. Phillips's claim, for example, that the "plantation was a school" where culture was disseminated from the top down.[170] In Freyre's interpretation of Brazilian slavery, culture was produced in the crossing of black and white.

As the anthropologist Peter Wade tells us, Freyre's positive view of racial mixture between black slaves and the Portuguese in Brazil represents an important phase in an intellectual trend that had begun in Latin America between 1850 and 1880. During this period and afterward, Latin American elites and intellectuals "struggled with the problem of how to understand and represent their emerging nations."[171] The end result was a construction of nationhood that recognized the mixed-race origins of Brazil, Cuba, Mexico, and some of the other states of Latin America and the Caribbean.[172] Recognizing that their origins were not totally European did not mean that these countries became avatars of racial egalitarianism or that all of their inhabitants accepted the idea of *mestizaje*. My intention here is not to argue that this process was not contested but rather to point out that *mestizaje* ultimately came to be seen as a central factor in these nations' origins. In short, these states were not, and do not understand themselves to be, communities "of common descent."[173]

Anyone familiar with the histories of Australia, Brazil, Canada, Colombia, Cuba, colonial Indonesia, Mexico, and South Africa knows that the history of the United States is not exceptional when it comes to the subject of interracial sex. Why some past American historians chose to make it so lies in the original concept of the state as an exemplar. But the work of more recent generations of historians indicates that this was never a white nation.[174] As Joel Williamson observed, when placed in a "world context and over centuries, the mixing of peoples of different colors and features that occurred in America was, of course, but a continuation of a process that is practically as old as the history of mankind."[175] In short, the myth of a white United States has to be abandoned and the Jeffersonian legacy broadened to include the idea that the Sage of Monticello was the father of our country in more ways than one.

Two | Character and History, or "Chloroform in Print"

I N THIS CHAPTER I focus on how the pre- and post-DNA discussions of Jefferson and Hemings have shaped and been shaped by our understanding of the racial origins and national identity of the American republic. I comment on and critique what both the pre- and post-DNA Jeffersonian hagiographers (those whom Gore Vidal has called "the Mount Rushmore biographers")[1] have had to say in their denials of the Jefferson-Hemings affair. What does their persistent refusal to accept what was already believed by some white Americans and by blacks generally, even before DNA corroboration, tell us about the state of contemporary American race relations? Equally important, what does it reveal about the way our nation's history, and that of its founders, has been constructed?

Nations require both myths of origin and mythic founders. Commenting on the difference between myth and history, Roland Barthes observed, "In passing from history to nature, myth acts economically: it abolishes the complexity of human acts, it gives them the simplicity of essences, it does away with all dialectics, with any going back beyond what is immediately visible, it organizes a world which is without contradictions because it is without depth, a world wide open and wallowing in the evident, it establishes a blissful charity: things appear to mean something by themselves."[2] In retrospect we can see how the mythic history of the United States was constructed around the identification of primitive "others," blacks and Native Americans, who could be presented, if they were mentioned at all, as a counterfoil to civilized white nation builders. Either ignored or marginalized, blacks and Native Americans thus posed no threat to the dominant fiction of progress and divine mission that was central to the history of the United States. As François Furstenberg has brilliantly shown, not only history but "popular writing shaped ideas of citizenship and nationalism."[3] In this literature, as Furstenberg shows, blacks passively accepted slavery and thus did not participate in the creation of the United States.[4]

The absence of black people in the master narrative of the nation's past was described by the black abolitionist and novelist William Wells Brown as resulting from white historians' having "thrown the colored man out."[5] Brown well understood that when the Founding Fathers created the American republic they framed a historical narrative for the nation that exclusively equated whiteness with progress, civilization, and citizenship. As Chief Justice Taney proclaimed in the Dred Scott case in 1856, "The founders knew that it [the Declaration] would not, in any part of the civilized world, be supposed to embrace the negro race, which by common consent, has been excluded from civilized governments and the family of nations, and doomed to slavery."[6] Because they were not part of the nation's genealogy, blacks had no place in its history. Black people, to quote the late Nathan Huggins, "did not exist in the world that mattered."[7] Here, for example, is the blunt pronouncement made in 1902 by the Atlanta editor John Temple Graves: "This is our country . . . we made it. We molded it. We control it, and we always will. We have done great things. We have mighty things yet to do. The Negro is an accident — an unwilling, a blameless, but an unwholesome, unwelcome, helpless, unassimilable element in our civilization. He is not made for our times."[8]

It is instructive to compare how American blacks were cast (or not cast) in the white-authored pageant of American history with how the Aborigines were perceived in another former British colony, Australia. There the master narrative, like that of the

United States, was constructed around the achievements of white settlers of British ancestry. In both cases the colonists or new people "fought the hierarchical order of the Old World to found a new egalitarian one."[9] Both tales of national origin were selective and racially referential in their depiction of the past based on *historicist* representations of nonwhites. The remarks of the Australian educator Walter Murdoch in a school primer published in 1917 echo and expand upon the sentiments of the Atlantan John Temple Graves fifteen years earlier:

> When people talk about "the history of Australia" they mean the history of white people who have lived in Australia. There is good reason why we should not stretch to make it include … the dark skinned wandering tribes who hurled boomerangs and ate snakes in their native land for long ages before the arrival of the first intruders from Europe … for they have nothing that can be called a history. They have dim legends, and queer fairy tales, and deep-rooted customs which have come down from long, long ago; but they have no history, as we use the word. When the white man came among them, he found them living just as their fathers and grandfathers and remote ancestors had lived before them. … Change and progress are the stuff of which history is made. These blacks knew no change and made no progress, as far as we can tell. Men of science [i.e., anthropologists] may peer at them … but the historian is not concerned with them. He is concerned with Australia only as the dwelling place of white men and women, settlers from overseas. It is his business to tell us how these white folk found the land, how they settled it, how they explored it, and how they gradually made it the Australia we know today.[10]

Commenting on the problem of historical silences, the anthropologist Michel-Rolph Trouillot wrote, "Silences enter the process of historical production at four crucial moments: the moment of fact creation (the making of sources), the moment of fact assembly (the making of archives), the moment of fact retrieval (the making of narratives), and the retrospective significance (the making of history in the final instance)."[11] The last two of these strategies constitute the principal sites of historical silence about America's racial and sexual past, and unease about America's racial and sexual past has given rise to a particular understanding of American history. "America," as Tony Judt has recently reminded us, is "an anxious country curiously detached from its own past as well as from the rest of the world and hungry for a fireside fairy tale with a happy ending."[12] This exercise in wish fulfillment has produced a historical narrative constructed around ideas emphasizing American exceptionalism. We now need to examine more closely how the canonical narrative history of the United States has been constructed, and by whom.

In his *Letters from an American Farmer*, published in 1782, Hector St. John de Crevecoeur described the populace of North America as a "mixture of Scotch, Irish, French, Dutch, German, and Swedes." "From this promiscuous breed," he went on to explain, "that race called American have arisen."[13] Writing in the 1920s about America's racial profile, those two icons of progressivism, Charles Austin Beard and Mary Ritter Beard, observed that Anglo-America had avoided the taint of miscegenation by preserving "its racial strains and not [fusing] with Indians and Negroes, as was the case in large parts of Spanish America."[14] Central to both Crevecoeur and the Beards' analyses was the assumption that European groups could mix and still retain the quality of whiteness, because these groups approximated each other in the scale of Caucasianism. Underlying this was the idea of "*filiation* — a linear, biological, grounded process that ties children to their parents."[15] Although the Irish and other immigrants might not have been initially accepted into the family of American whiteness, the presence of blacks created a racial logic that resulted in this eventuality. This is what Milton M.

Gordon meant many years ago when he described the process of European assimilation in America as "Anglo Conforming."[16] Gordon asked whether it was not possible, then, "to think of the evolving American society not simply as a slightly modified England but rather as a totally new blend, culturally and biologically, in which the stocks and folkways of Europe were, figuratively speaking, indiscriminately mixed in the political pot of the emerging nation and melted together by the fires of American influence and interaction into a distinctly new type."[17] Notably absent from this pot were Native Americans and blacks.

In promulgating the fantasy of an imagined whiteness unblemished by either amalgamation or miscegenation, the Beards were only expressing a sensibility that was pervasive in their day among white Americans. Although this attitude has mellowed, it has not totally disappeared. For many Americans, even in the twenty-first century, white and black are bifurcated racial categories and in no way mixed. As one of my students recently told me, he knew a black or white person when he saw one, and my emphasis on the social construction of race was "bullshit." The reality, however, is that most blacks in the United States "are on average about 17 percent white; they have mitochondria (maternally inherited) that are African, but they often have European Y chromosomes."[18] The reality of this intermixture was captured by antebellum New York free Negroes when they observed that their ancestry was diverse: "We trace it to Englishmen, Irishmen, Scotchmen; to the German; to the Asiatic, as well as to Africa. The best blood of Virginia courses through our veins."[19] These black people were not engaging in hyperbole when they claimed Virginian ancestry. The duc de La Rochefoucauld-Liancourt, one of the most discerning commentators on American society, observed in the 1790s that white planters feared that the presence of emancipated slaves in the Chesapeake would threaten the purity of white bloodlines. "In future generations, they say," reported the French nobleman, "there would not be a countenance to be seen without more or less of the black color."[20] The slave girl Harriet Jacobs captured the racial transformation of black people when she asked, "Who can measure the amount of Anglo-Saxon blood coursing in the veins of American slaves?"[21]

Although both Charles and Mary Beard were perceptive students of American manners and mores, their comments about the racial provenance of the American people exemplify the racial and sexual amnesia and unease that have historically characterized most white and some black Americans' disquietude about interracial sex and the attendant misperception that the "visible" is an "epistemological guarantee" of whiteness or blackness.[22] They may also have failed to consider the role that race or racial mixture played in the history of the United States because Charles Beard had deep reservations about the future of blacks in American society and was not sanguine about "the innate capacity of colored [people] to throw off [their] shiftlessness and indifference to high standards of life."[23] For an earlier generation of American historians, including the Beards, slavery "was an episode" and its destruction removed a barrier to the economic progress of the United States.[24] Once slavery, an impediment to national progress, was obliterated, blacks were expected to remain a separate servitor class.[25] Although the Beards and other historians of their generation — unlike Thomas Jefferson and Samuel Sewall — were at least reconciled to blacks' permanent presence in America, they nevertheless were unwilling to acknowledge them as full members of American society or to recognize their presence in the American gene pool.

Blacks, because of their history of powerlessness in America, have been forced to confront the issue of interracial sex in ways their white fellow countrymen have not. Whereas many black families during slavery and since have incorporated the products of amalgamation/miscegenation into their ranks,[26] more often than not white families have either denied their blackness or have been forced to acknowledge some touch of "the tar" only when the evidence became undeniable. Before moving on to examine the case of Thomas Jefferson and Sally Hemings, it would be useful to examine several others that have left their traces in the historical record.

There is, for example, the case of John Catron, the first chief justice of the Tennessee Supreme Court, who refused to acknowledge his child by a slave woman, Sally. Catron's mulatto son, James Thomas, writing in his autobiography, did not remember his father fondly. "Now my own father was the Hon C and filled chairs of distinction.... He presided over the supreme court (of Tennessee) ten years but he had no time to give me a thought. He gave me twenty five cents once. If I was correctly informed that was all he ever did for me."[27] Catron, who ultimately became a justice of the United States Supreme Court, never acknowledged Thomas as his son.

Another high-profile white southern politician with a mixed-race child, this time from the recent past, was Strom Thurmond, the late Republican senator from South Carolina. Although Thurmond, like Catron, managed to go to his grave without acknowledging his paternity, he was publicly "outed" after his death by his daughter. Thurmond's white family responded with disbelief and a profound sense of shame to the revelation that the Dixiecrat had fathered a mulatto child in his youth.[28] How was this possible given Thurmond's publicly stated position, when he was governor of South Carolina, that "segregation laws [are] essential to the racial purity of the white and Negro races alike"?[29] When Essie Mae Washington-Williams went public with her parentage, one of her father's nieces said that her cousin's revelation "was like a blight on the family." Exposure of the transgression made it difficult for another member of the Thurmond family to appear in public: "I went to a church meeting the other day and all of these people came up to me and you could tell they didn't know what to say. For the first time in my life, I felt shame."[30]

Not every liaison between a white man and a black woman was

as fleeting as those involving John Catron and Strom Thurmond. Nor was every white father of mixed-race children unwilling to involve himself in their upbringing. There was, for example, the case of the Georgia planter Nathan Sayre. During the 1830s Sayre constructed the mansion Pomegranate Hall in Sparta, Georgia, complete with a secret apartment for his "free colored mistress, Susan Hunt, and their three children." Over the course of a quarter-century, while Sayre became prominent in Georgia politics, he and his lover "raised children in the hidden home behind Pomegranate's false walls as Sayre publicly maintained a fictional bachelorhood." Sayre's relatives and neighbors conspired in the "charade ... turning a blind eye, the secret was complete."[31] Evidently the white Sayre relatives were complicit in protecting the secret of Nathan Sayre's interracial family. For his part, by going to such elaborate lengths to keep his lover and their children concealed, Sayre implicitly acknowledged that there was something shameful going on that should decently be concealed. In a very concrete way, he constructed a space of silence within his house.

In considering these case histories, it is important to note that for these white men and their families the shame lay not in their fathering illegitimate children but in their fathering children of mixed race. Had Strom Thurmond's secret daughter been white, according to his niece, "it would be a whole other situation, because public criticism would not have been as harsh."[32] Bastardy is something white men can be forgiven, as I have written elsewhere. What shame, for example, did either Benjamin Franklin or Grover Cleveland experience after it was made public that they had fathered children out of wedlock? "While some might hold these indiscretions against them, the crossing of racial boundaries would have been more damaging still. Franklin and Cleveland were just 'sowing wild oats,' or, as the saying goes, 'boys being boys.' But had these two white men produced mixed-race children, the magnitude of their indiscretions would have increased markedly. Miscegenation, not bastardy, would be the issue foremost in the minds of their critics."[33]

Although his reputation took a serious blow from his daughter's revelations, Strom Thurmond, of course, was beyond the reach of any direct political damage when the truth of his relationship with Carrie Butler finally came out. The consequences of being publicly identified with miscegenation during one's active political life could be far more damaging, however. For a prime example of this we can look to the life of Richard M. Johnson, of Kentucky, a hero of the War of 1812 who was Martin Van Buren's vice president. For decades, Johnson (who never legally married) openly cohabited as common-law husband with Julie Chinn, an octoroon slave woman, on his farm in Kentucky. Together the couple had two daughters, whom Johnson publicly acknowledged. When Johnson's daughters grew up, he married them to white men and presented each of them with land.[34] Eventually, the repercussions of this openly unorthodox behavior ended his political career.

Richard M. Johnson occupied a place on the national stage, but it was not a uniquely prominent or distinguished one. The fact that he openly had sex with a slave woman and fathered mixed-race children would never have threatened the very foundation myth of the United States or the self-image of many Americans. For stakes this high, we must return to the case of Thomas Jefferson and Sally Hemings.

Whiteness as an ideologically constructed racial subjectivity requires a Jefferson who did not blot the escutcheon of whiteness.[35] Uniting the pre- and post-DNA discussion of Thomas Jefferson and Sally Hemings is a "reasoned outcome" argument.[36] I will have more to say about what I mean by a reasoned outcome shortly. This defense has been complicated by the 1998 publication of the DNA test results,[37] but in many ways it has remained essentially the same.

It's Unthinkable: He Didn't Do It
Because He Couldn't Have Done It

Gore Vidal, quoting Jefferson's hagiographers, captures the third president's place in the nation's racial history with this comment: "No gentleman would have gone to bed with a slave. Since Thomas Jefferson was the greatest gentleman of his period, he could not have done so either. That takes care of that."[38] To see Jefferson "as the all-too-human father of a mixed-race country," as Scot French has noted, has been "unthinkable" for a number of white professional historians and others.[39] How could Jefferson have been a participant in what Benedict Anderson, writing in another context, has called "loathsome copulation"?[40] Historians such as Douglass Adair, Dumas Malone, Alf J. Mapp Jr., John Chester Miller, Merrill D. Peterson, and Willard Sterne Randall, to name a few, have expended a great deal of ink trying to prove that he could not.[41] These scholars defined character in a particularly narrow way. They knew what they meant and hoped their readers would have a corresponding belief, namely, that interracial sex was bad and engaging in it was a sign of loss of character or moral situatedness, which could never befall a Founding Father. In the legal world, this position might be called a "reasoned outcome": the affair never happened because it could not have happened. Annette Gordon-Reed summarizes this position as follows: "The underlying theme of most historians' denial of the truth of a liaison between Thomas Jefferson and Sally Hemings is that the whole story is too impossible to believe. This line of argument is troubling. For in order to sustain the claim of impossibility, or even to discuss the matter in those terms, one has to make Thomas Jefferson so high as to have been something more than human and one has to make Sally Hemings so low as to have been something less than human."[42]

John Chester Miller expressed this dubious sensibility when he wrote in 1977 that "for Jefferson to have conducted a love affair with a slave woman and to have raised his children as slaves is completely at variance with his character, in so far as it can be determined by his acts and words, the strict moral code by which he professed to live and which he constantly enjoined upon others, especially men and women, and his conception of women and their place in society."[43] Miller's position echoes that of his eminent predecessor, the Pulitzer Prize–winning Jefferson biographer Dumas Malone. In Malone's view, a Jefferson-Hemings liaison would have signaled moral deficiency and the betrayal of family honor in a man who, by his definition, was incapable of such lapses. "It is virtually inconceivable," he wrote, "that this fastidious gentleman whose devotion to his dead wife's memory and to the happiness of his daughters and grand-children bordered on the excessive could have carried on through a period of years a vulgar liaison which his own family could not fail to detect."[44]

This "it's unthinkable" defense of Jefferson is based upon both his chaste devotion to his dead wife and his borderline-excessive devotion to his family. Malone also used the word *devotion* several times in describing Jefferson's relationship to his wife and other family members in an informal 1976 lecture to the members of the Monticello Association in which he proposed to "talk to you informally about Mr. Jefferson as a family man." To these white lineal descendants of Jefferson, Malone spoke fulsomely of their progenitor: "I don't need to remind you that Mr. Jefferson was very much a family man. He had many sides to his character, but there's none that is more attractive than the domestic side." He went on to say that "it would be hard to fault Mr. Jefferson's conduct as a family man" and that "he was a devoted family man in every respect."[45] Within the friendly confines of the Monticello Association, Malone had no need to spell out to his listeners his conviction that no one with such an attractive and devoted domestic side could imaginably have been making babies with a black slave woman at the same time that he lovingly indulged his daughters and their offspring and cherished the memory of his wife. Yet, as we have already seen, Malone was quite prepared to push the point all the way home and deploy this same image of Jefferson's chastity and extreme familial devotion in the service of refuting the Sally Hemings charge. In this he was following the lead of none other than Jefferson's own Randolph grandchildren. In a famous letter to her husband in 1858, Ellen Randolph Coolidge had this to say: "I put it to any fair mind to decide if a man so admirable to his domestic character as Mr. Jefferson, so devoted to his daughters and their children, so fond of their society, so tender, considerate, refined in his intercourse with them, so watchful over them in all respects, would be likely to rear a race of half-breeds under their eyes and carry on his low amours in the circle of his family."[46] In a conversation reported years later by the Jefferson historian and kinsman Henry S. Randall, Coolidge's brother, Thomas Jefferson Randolph, reportedly characterized his grandfather in defending him against the Hemings allegation as "chaste and pure — as 'immaculate a man as God ever created.'"[47]

If we deconstruct the defense used by Malone and Miller in the twentieth century and Jefferson's family members Ellen Randolph Coolidge and her brother in the nineteenth, we find two closely connected strands to the argument. One is that Jefferson would never have polluted his family home and the environs of his children and grandchildren by engaging in "a vulgar liaison" (Malone) or "low amours" (Coolidge) that would produce a "race of half-breeds" (Coolidge). The other is that Jefferson, who was "devoted to his wife" (Malone), who lived by a "strict moral code" (Miller), who was "chaste and pure" (Randolph), who showed "devotion to his dead wife's memory" (Malone), and who had a clearly exalted "conception of women and their place in society" (Miller), could never have felt the need for sex after his wife died. The idea that Jefferson had a sex life after his wife's death is "unthinkable."

Unlike other nations, where the sexuality of leaders, both past and present, is treated with a degree of tolerance and detachment, white America, with its heritage of ersatz Victorian sexual sensibility, has long regarded this as something to be ashamed of rather than acknowledged. Some white Americans have a very hard time thinking about their leaders with their pants down. Their highly limited interpretations of Jefferson as a sexual animal reflect a limited, ultimately distorted understanding of white male sexuality, particularly in the eighteenth century, which is forgivable perhaps in the informal comments of family members but far less so in the work of professional historians. In their efforts to moralize about Jefferson, Malone, Miller, and others constructed a twentieth-century white male bourgeois fantasy rooted in a particular time and moment in the history of American race and sexual relations. Michel Foucault called this type of unexamined historical scholarship "knowledge as perspective."[48]

Deeply ingrained in historians' denials of the Jefferson-Hemings liaison is an invariant notion of sexuality. Reading their own present into the past, these men never stopped to consider that eighteenth-century sexual practice was different from that in the nineteenth and twentieth centuries. Commenting on this problem in the study of sex, the sociologist Gail Hawkes cautions against reading the eighteenth century as the nineteenth: "The nineteenth century elements in modernist sexuality are distinct from those of the century that preceded it, most notably in the loss of the brief 'moment' of fundamental celebration of sexual pleasure. Though circumscribed, as we have seen, eighteenth-century society loved (heterosexual) sex and its pleasures and indulged in them with a minimum of guilt and anxiety."[49] As Hawkes goes on to note, the nineteenth century saw a transition from the more casual and open attitudes toward sex of the eighteenth century:

Nineteenth-century attitudes to sexual pleasure were very different. Overall they represented the opposite of Enlightenment

enthusiasm. . . . If the prevailing characteristic of the eighteenth century was one of affirmation, that of the nineteenth
century was one of fear and distrust of excessive indulgence.
In this it reflected the social ethic that drove capitalism to its
maturity. There was in the nineteenth century an ethos of
economy and of rationality of all practice in all areas of life.
Sober self-control in relation to sensual pleasures was the defining feature of the bourgeois social order. Sexual pleasure
was subjugated to considerations of individual purpose and
social outcomes.[50]

Implicit in the "it's unthinkable" defense is the idea that no truly
loving family man could have an erotic life outside the domestic
circle. That this is not so can be seen in *The Commonplace Book* of
William Byrd II, private musings by an early Virginia colonial and
part-time Londoner who died the year after Jefferson's birth. As
the editors of *The Commonplace Book* point out, "Byrd's attitude
toward sexuality . . . was fully compartmentalized, divided into
clearly demarcated categories." Nor did Byrd's behavior produce
cognitive dissonance: "There was no indication anywhere that
Byrd experienced any sense of personal inconsistency at living in
two separate realms of experience, erotic indulgence and high romance."[51] In studying Jefferson, historians should be equally willing to compartmentalize, to avoid conflating things that should
remain separate. In the first place, they have to move beyond assertions that on her deathbed Jefferson's wife extracted "a promise
that [he] would never put their children under the care of a step
mother."[52] If Jefferson made such a promise, it did not mean that
he became celibate. Remarriage is one thing; sex is another. It is
foolish, if not naive, to think that a sexually active and mature man
would live the rest of his life as a monk.

Moreover, because Jefferson's relationships with Martha Wayles
and Sally Hemings do not occupy the same analytical space, one

cannot be used to deny the possibility of the other. His affection for his wife in life and his devotion to her memory in death have no bearing on his willingness to enter into a relationship with his concubine. Analyzing what Jefferson was or was not capable of doing requires a far more complex reading of his sexuality and its historical context than his defenders have been willing to accept.

The studies of Jefferson written by Malone and others like him typify the limits of biography and the examination of the lives of great men that Sigmund Freud cautioned against in his biographical study *Leonardo da Vinci and a Memory of His Childhood,* published in 1910.[53] Freud's study is worth quoting at some length because his comment about the limitations of some types of biography speaks to the silences and denials present in the Jefferson scholarship dealing with Sally Hemings. "If a biographic study is really intended to arrive at an understanding of its hero's mental life," wrote Freud, "it must not — as happens in the majority of biographies as a result of discretion or prudishness — silently pass over its subject's sexual activity or individuality." Authors who wrote such books, Freud said, "tolerate [in their subjects] no vestige of human weakness or imperfection.... They present us with what is in fact a cold, strange, ideal figure instead of a human being to whom we might feel ourselves distantly related.... They thereby sacrifice truth to an illusion, and for the sake of their infantile fantasies abandon the opportunity of penetrating the most fascinating secrets of human nature."[54]

In the same way that the apologists were consciously out to protect Jefferson, unconsciously they were out to perfect an ideal model of the nuclear family. Character and family values were deployed to protect Jefferson's reputation and assimilate him into "the grand narrative of connubiality."[55] Bent on saving his hero from the scurrilous, Dumas Malone created a Jefferson who was a "consistently temperate man." Malone failed to take into account that people often lie about their sex lives; it is difficult for most humans,

Founding Fathers or not, to be candid about this aspect of their lives. Thus, when Malone wrote that sex with Hemings would have been "distinctly out of character, being virtually unthinkable in a man of Jefferson's moral standards and habitual conduct," I think he told his readers more about himself than about Jefferson.[56]

The (White) Family Would Have Known

A second line of argument, again used by both Jefferson's family and professional apologists, is that if Jefferson had been carrying on a long-term liaison that produced one or several mixed-race children, his white children and grandchildren would have known. Dumas Malone assumed that Jefferson's family "failed to detect" any "vulgar liaison" with Hemings and that this supported his claim that the liaison never existed.[57] John Chester Miller asserted that Jefferson's daughters "were not aware of their father's alleged relations with Sally Hemings."[58] If this is true, they may have been engaging in a process of denial that Mary Boykin Chestnut described in her diary when she wrote that "daughters in their purity and innocence are supposed never to dream of what is as plain before their eyes as the sunlight, and they play their parts of unsuspecting angels to the letter. They prefer to adore their father as model of all earthly goodness."[59]

This attitude of denial was shared by a later generation of Jeffersons of both sexes. For example, Jefferson's grandson Thomas Jefferson Randolph claimed to have slept so close at hand to Jefferson at Monticello that he would surely have detected any stealthy goings-on between Jefferson and Hemings. Randolph told the nineteenth-century historian Henry S. Randall that he had never seen a suspicious "look, or a motion, or a circumstance."[60] To his sister, Randolph "positively declare[d] his indignant belief in the imputations and solemnly affirm[ed] that he never saw or heard the smallest thing which could lead him to suspect that his grandfather's life was other than perfectly pure."[61]

The two Jefferson family members who are on record as having directly denied the Jefferson-Hemings affair are Ellen Randolph Coolidge and her brother, Thomas Jefferson Randolph, both children of Jefferson's elder daughter, Martha. The Randolph branch of the family was particularly well acquainted with life at Monticello since Martha and her children lived there after Jefferson's retirement and her son later managed Jefferson's business affairs. In terms of close physical proximity, the Randolphs were certainly well-placed witnesses. Evidently, the Hemings allegations were discussed within the family. Henry Randall's letter recounting his conversation with Thomas Jefferson Randolph states that Martha Jefferson Randolph "took the Dusky Sally stories much to heart" and describes an occasion shortly before her death in which she used the record of Monticello slave births to drive home to them that they must always "defend the character of their grandfather."[62] In Ellen Randolph Coolidge's letter to her husband she writes that "I have been talking freely with my brother Jefferson on the subject of the 'yellow children' and will give you the substance of our conversation, with my subsequent reflections." Coolidge goes on to ask, disingenuously, "How comes it that [Jefferson's] immoralities were never suspected by his own family — that his daughter and her children rejected with horror and contempt the charges brought against him[?]"[63] Here lies the crux of the matter. Was the issue that they did not know, or was there a desire not to know because, as the French film director Michael Haneke stated in another context, "the personal is often hidden in the home"?[64] What did the Jefferson children and grandchildren suppress in order to maintain their social position and the reputation of their famous progenitor? What did they deny, perhaps even to themselves?

Family is the site for the reproduction of power, and both denial and repression are expressions or manifestations of familial power. Certainly this was the case in the 1790s, when Richard Randolph, a cousin of Thomas Jefferson's, allegedly fathered a child by his sister-in-law, Nancy, and then murdered the baby after its birth. The Randolphs used their considerable power to exonerate Richard and temporarily maintain the family's reputation. Ultimately, as Cynthia Kierner shows, it was the gossip slaves passed on to poor whites, which was then told to the aristocracy, that brought Randolph to trial.[65] Within the Jefferson household there must have been some covert discussion of the Jefferson-Hemings relationship among the house slaves. The fact that there is no written record of these conversations does not mean they did not occur. Nor is it clear that the Jefferson children and grandchildren did not hear the servants' discussions about the affair. Children and adolescents see and are aware of family secrets even when they are not discussed publicly. If it is true that parents know things that their children do not know, the reverse is also true.

Implicit in the children-did-not-know argument is a notion of childhood innocence that was not prevalent in society before the nineteenth century. The idea of childhood innocence is a product of the late eighteenth century and the rise of romanticism. Commenting on the presumption of sexual innocence in a different time and place, Guido Ruggiero cautioned against assuming that "sexual innocence for the young [extended] to a presumption of sexual ignorance. The distinction is an important one. The modern assumption of a virtual equation of ignorance and innocence was just not feasible in the [eighteenth century]."[66] The Jefferson children and grandchildren grew up in a world in which a host of human activities were more public than they would be in the nineteenth and twentieth centuries. This was particularly true for people living in rural settings. Young girls living in both the Virginia countryside and Paris in the eighteenth century knew much more about sex than white middle-class male historians writing in the first half of the twentieth century, who were shaped by a more repressed nineteenth-century sexual sensibility.

Jefferson's children and grandchildren, moreover, were part of a family in which there was a tradition of white men "sleeping black." Could they have been unaware of the fact that Martha Wayles Jefferson's father was Sally's progenitor and that Sally was her half-sister? And what of Martha herself? How did this eighteenth-century upper-class white woman process her father's relationship with a slave woman? Did she steel herself, as Martha Custis Washington did, against white society's belief that her father's behavior was unseemly? Martha Washington had a half-sister named Ann Dandridge, the child of Martha's father and an unknown slave woman of "mixed white, Native American, African blood" whom she kept as a slave.[67] Henry Wiencek, writing about the relationship between Martha Washington and her black half-sister, captures the multiple layers of contradiction that characterized the master-slave relationship when he describes "the capacity of the masters and mistresses to tolerate profound psychological dislocation, the conversion of kin into property."[68]

To return to Ellen Randolph Coolidge's tendentious question —"How comes it that . . . his daughter and her children rejected with horror and contempt the charges brought against him[?]"— from their point of view Jefferson's family had good cause to react with horror and contempt, and still better cause to reject the charges. This does not, however, mean that the charges were not true or that the family knew they were.

What Dumas Malone and his peers failed to acknowledge was the silences that exist in families about the failures of patriarchs, brothers, and sons. Writing in a world in which the family was conceived of as a haven from the unseemly, these historians failed to acknowledge that families and communities are often silent about or conspire to cover up activities that might be defined as criminal. Within the white community, this is particularly true of issues involving race (amalgamation/miscegenation) and lynching, as some recent studies have shown.[69] Writing in another context, the literary critic D. A. Miller labeled this type of secret "the open secret, the secret that everybody knows."[70] The response of Jefferson's white family can only be understood when it is placed in a context in which family is not idealized but is seen as a site where power is produced. By either being silent or claiming that other, less exalted male Jeffersons had fathered Hemings's children, the family protected its name and honor.

Living in a world where public discussion or recognition of interracial sex was distasteful and dishonorable, the Jeffersons felt compelled to exempt the Sage of Monticello from this form of social interaction. Their efforts, and those of the historians who followed their lead, created the central component of the myth of Jefferson the family man and Founding Father. This tale is grounded in the fictive space where most heterosexual men supposedly live with the love of wives and children. In the case of Jefferson, this fiction constitutes an example of the "personal being extended to the national."[71] Framing this tale is the fiction of a wholesome, pristine institution — family — where monogamy and racial lines are always intact. But the racial and sexual history of America, as I have been suggesting, can offer neither black nor white people much assurance on this point. This is what makes the canonical interpretation of Jefferson both before and after 1998 problematic.

Somebody Else Did It

No one seems prepared to deny that some of the slaves at Monticello bore a striking resemblance to the Sage himself and that the presence of these look-alikes led people to speculate about their paternity. The archdenier Thomas Jefferson Randolph was refreshingly candid on that score. Here is how Henry S. Randall reported his remarks on the subject:

There was a better excuse for [the allegations] said he, than you might think: she had children which resembled Mr. Jefferson so closely that it was plain that they had his blood in their veins. He said in one case that the resemblance was so close, that at some distance or in the dusk the slave, dressed in . the same way, might be mistaken for Mr. Jefferson. He said in one instance, a gentleman dining with Mr. Jefferson looked so startled as he raised his eyes from the latter to the servant behind him, that his discovery of the resemblance was perfectly obvious to all. Sally Henings [sic] was a house servant and her children were brought up house servants — so that the likeness between master and slave was blazoned to all the multitudes who visited this political Mecca.[72]

The obvious solution to this awkward problem was to construe the father of the Hemings children, not as Jefferson himself, but as someone closely enough related to Jefferson to explain the family resemblance. Randolph had a ready candidate, or rather two of them, in the form of Jefferson's nephews Peter and Samuel Carr: "Col. Randolph," reported Henry Randall, "informed me that Sally Henings [sic] was the mistress of Peter, and her sister Betsey the mistress of Samuel — and from these connections sprang the progeny which resembled Jefferson." Randolph's sister, Ellen Randolph Coolidge, proposed a variation of this same explanation, although she reassigned the paternity of Sally Hemings's children to Samuel: "The four children of Sally Hemmings [sic] were all the children of Col. Carr, the notorious and good natured Turk that ever was master of a black seraglio kept at other men's expense."[73] Although it is taken at face value by Jefferson apologists, this letter is actually a racist fantasy constructed around, on the one hand, an ideal white man (Jefferson) who is restrained around white women and, on the other hand, a white man (Carr) who is promiscuous in his relations with enslaved women.[74] Coolidge's use of the terms

Turk and *seraglio* echoes the imagery of the 1828 pornographic novel *The Lustful Turk,* in which the Turk is a ravisher of European women and insatiable in his sexual appetites. In Europe, the Turk served the same psychosexual function as a sexual alter ego for nineteenth-century Englishmen as blacks did for American whites in both the North and the South preceding the Civil War.[75] In both cases the sexualized "other" constituted libido out of control. It is this sensibility that informs Coolidge's characterization of Carr.

The tradition ascribing paternity to one of the Carr brothers was revived after the Hemings-Jefferson story gained new prominence in the mid-twentieth century. Both historians and white Jefferson descendants eager to discredit the allegations turned once again to Jefferson's nephews to deal with what Alfred Mapp Jr. called "the undeniable fact that some of [Hemings's] children resembled Jefferson and other members of his family" and the "specious credence" this resemblance lent to the allegations about Jefferson's paternity.[76] Douglass Adair went so far as to posit a long-running romance between Sally Hemings and Peter Carr, accepting their relationship as a given and describing it as a "love match."[77]

Unfortunately for the Carr proponents, the DNA testing found no genetic link between the Hemings descendants and the Carr descendants, conclusively ruling out both of Jefferson's nephews and debunking the claims of the Randolph grandchildren. Jefferson apologists then turned their attention to another family member, Thomas's brother, Randolph, whose shared patrilineal descent with his brother gives him equal footing with Thomas in terms of DNA evidence as a possible Hemings progenitor. Randolph got the post-DNA endorsement of the Thomas Jefferson Heritage Society, which, among its stated goals, aims "to stand always in opposition to those who would seek to undermine the integrity of Thomas Jefferson,"[78] and of the commission of scholars the society convened for a post-DNA investigation of the evidence. Supporters of the Randolph-did-it theory are in some difficulty, however, when it comes to explaining why their candidate was not implicated by the Randolph grandchildren, by other nineteenth-century commentators, or by historians before the Carrs were ruled out by science.[79]

Pay No Attention to Those Black People Over There in the Corner

Post-DNA Jefferson apologists are quick to point out that because of the limitations of DNA testing, Jefferson cannot be conclusively identified as Eston Hemings's father. The Carrs were ruled out; Jefferson was ruled in, along with several others in the same male line. Still, Jefferson was ruled in. Along with this inconvenient truth, his post-DNA defenders also have to contend with a legacy of oral and written testimony to the affair that dates back more than two hundred years. They deal with it in the same way that Jefferson apologists always have done: by impugning its sources.

One of the most important pieces of testimony about Hemings and Jefferson was the interview with Hemings's son Madison published in the *Pike County Republican* in 1873. In the interview, Madison identified Jefferson as not only his own father but the father of all his siblings.[80] Five days later the editor of a rival newspaper published a savage rebuttal, claiming that it was "a well known peculiarity of the colored race" to "lay claim to illustrious parentage" and that slave mothers had habitually lied to their children about their fathers because "it sounds much better for the mother to tell her offspring that 'master' is their father than to acknowledge to them that some field hand, without a name, had raised her to the dignity of a mother."[81] Several months later, the *Pike County Republican* published an interview with Israel Jefferson, a former slave at Monticello, that corroborated Madison Hemings's account.[82] This time, none other than Thomas Jefferson Randolph himself leapt to his grandfather's defense. In a letter to the newspaper he claimed, among other things, that because of their "bitter, bitter jealousy"

of the Hemings family, the other Monticello slaves were unwilling
to attribute the Hemingses' high status to its true cause, which was
"very superior intelligence capacity and fidelity to trusts," and that
therefore they spread tales about Jefferson's paternity.[83] After the
Madison Hemings interview resurfaced in the 1950s, Jefferson historians used similar arguments. Merrill D. Peterson, for example,
dismissed the black oral tradition about Jefferson and Hemings
as a case of "the Negroes' pathetic wish for a little pride."[84] All of
these specious explanations rest upon the same racist assumption,
expressed here by the observation of John Burgess, of Columbia
University, that "the Negro had no pride of race and no aspirations
or ideals save to be like whites."[85]

In her book *Thomas Jefferson and Sally Hemings* Annette
Gordon-Reed masterfully deconstructs the efforts to discredit
Madison Hemings.[86] Gordon-Reed explodes the idea that Hemings was a black man so devoid of self-esteem that he had to fab-
ricate a relationship between the third president and his mother
to assert his humanity and place in American history. But there
is a larger problem here than just the issue of Madison Hemings's
testimony, namely, the problem of who owns history.[87] If, as James
Baldwin once wrote, "the cultural pretensions of history are revealed as nothing less than a mask for power,"[88] then the entire
debate about Jefferson and Hemings has to be seen as an expression of white male power to define the racial origins and national
identity of the American republic. Because black is an invention
of whiteness, it was easy for whites to dismiss the claims of Madison Hemings and other blacks about Jefferson as unsubstantiated
and, more generally, to reject black memory and oral tradition. The
black story was disparaged because it was unthinkable.

These denials are examples of the narrative strategy that I previously called the "reasoned outcome." The problem with the reasoned outcome, writes Gordon-Reed, is "that the scholars [and
others] who fashioned Jefferson's image were either unwilling or

unable to weigh the matter objectively. This did not stop them, however, from writing as if they had done so."[89] Claiming to know Jefferson based on their reading of his personal correspondence and state papers, the historians who rejected the possibility of a sexual relationship between Jefferson and Hemings erected a cordon sanitaire around his reputation. The creation of this defense involved, as E. M. Halliday has written, a form of projection on the part of Malone and Peterson (and, of course, many others): "The two scholars seem to have constructed an image of their hero pleasantly consonant with their view of themselves as liberal-minded but socially conservative Virginia gentlemen, and judged his relationship with Sally Hemings accordingly."[90]

It is dangerous to project oneself back into the past. Historians can identify with their subjects, but they should exercise a bifocality; that is, they should stand both inside and outside the period and context they are writing about in order to maintain a certain degree of fairness. On the subject of Jefferson and Hemings, Malone and Peterson and their peers wrote a history that was "hagiographic rather than historical, exemplary rather than analytical."[91] Enthralled by documentary evidence that they read in an unnuanced fashion, these historians did not attempt to move beyond what their documents said when it came to Jefferson's racial and sexual attitudes — as though Jefferson's writings somehow magically captured the past and did not require further interrogation for silences or misrepresentations. This can be seen in the canonization of queries 6 and 14 in *Notes on the State of Virginia* as Jefferson's ultimate statement on race. But American historians should heed the caution of the great French historian Lucien Fefebvre, who, in response to a document-driven methodology, observed that "there is no history; only historians."[92] According to the historian of religion Elizabeth A. Clark, Fefebvre meant that "it is the historian (not documents) who poses questions and hypotheses."[93] This is particularly true of some books written about great men and their thoughts, because involved in their construction is an evidentiary selection process that results in the creation of heroes. And nowhere is this more evident than in most of the texts written about the white founders of the United States.

Deeply influenced by a racism that effaced any evidence of black people's agency in the history of the American republic, white apologists for Jefferson "knew" that Jefferson could not have slept with Hemings and that black people's testimony to that effect was unreliable. This came as no surprise to black Americans, who perceived that whites, as the sharecropper Nate Shaw once remarked, "disrecognized them."[94] The black novelist Ralph Ellison illuminated this phenomenon when he wrote that "I am invisible, understand, simply because people refuse to see me. Like the bodiless heads you see sometimes in a circus side show, it is as though I have been surrounded by mirrors of hard distorting glass. When they approach they see only my surroundings, themselves, or figments of their imagination — indeed, everything and anything except me."[95] What the pre-DNA white historians and many other whites of their time saw was simply a category called "Negro." And although they claimed to know blacks, their perceptions of black people were deeply grounded in a racist paternalism that made the idea of Jefferson and Hemings unthinkable. As one old black woman once remarked, "To white people your colored person is always a stranger."[96] For the white men of Mapp, Malone, Miller, and Peterson's generation, black people were, if not invisible, certainly not worthy of consideration as historical actors. Focused on the life of a great man, they wrote a history that ignored blacks and reassured whites.

No subordinated population is ever totally socialized by its oppressor, however. The oppressed write histories of their past. This was true of the Jews in ancient Egypt and also of blacks in America, who began writing histories of their accomplishments in the eighteenth century.[97] The history they wrote has operated as a counternarrative to the dominant Whiggish interpretation of the American past, with its emphasis on the inexorable unfolding of freedom and the triumph of democratic institutions. In contrast, blacks wrote a history that challenged the smug and unproblematic understanding of the American past written by earlier generations of white historians. "People," as Henry Louis Gates Jr. has recently reminded us, "arrive at an understanding of themselves and the world through narratives. . . . Counter narratives are, in turn, the means by which groups contest the dominant reality and the fretwork of assumptions that supports it. Sometimes delusion lies in that way; sometimes not."[98] The black belief that Jefferson was the father of Hemings's children was not a delusion. It was grounded in a reality called slavery, in which men of the master class, regardless of their color, have always sexually exploited the women of the enslaved. To take note of this is neither prurient nor defamatory. Rather than viewing the oral testimony, memories, and novels of blacks as some sort of wishful thinking, we must understand these pieces of cultural production as contestation of the dominant.[99]

One of the more interesting aspects of interaction between whites and blacks in the United States is the tendency of some white people, not all, to tell blacks that they are exaggerating or misperceiving reality when they say something is racist. The black literary scholar Dwight McBride captures the bankruptcy of this strategy when commenting on how blacks and whites interact when talking about racism. McBride is worth quoting at some length on this subject. He says of a white friend that his

> disinclination to believe [me] was amazing. But his ability to call up so readily the rhetorical form that his disbelief assumed signaled to me that something in our societal ways of thinking about black people had not only brought us to a place where this gesture was commonplace, but also where the logic undergirding it could be viewed as neither slanderous or offensive.

Such logic operates on an implied gross fundamental fallacy, of course. That is, if the people who are the obvious victims of particular forms of discrimination (in this case racism) are also the most readily disqualified as witnesses to those same forms of discrimination, then according to such logic only those people who are not victimized by racism (i.e., whites) are the ones who are, indeed, the best and most reliable witness and judges to what actually happens to those racialized "others" in our society.[100]

That black people had been slaves and that amalgamation and miscegenation were a part of bondage in Albermarle County and other slaveholding regions meant nothing when it came to defending Jefferson and discrediting people like Madison Hemings. Because blacks were not serious historical actors, their understanding of the widespread practice of amalgamation/miscegenation was not taken seriously.

In some quarters it still is not. This tradition of disparagement has survived virtually intact into the twenty-first century. Here is what historian David Mayer, a member of the commission of scholars, has to say:

There are many reasons to doubt the reliability of the oral tradition handed down by the Madison Hemings' descendants. Significantly, there is no evidence of an oral tradition corroborating the assertions attributed to Madison Hemings which antedates the publication of the 1873 *Pike County Republican* story. Thus, rather than being an oral history handed down to her descendants by Sally Hemings herself — or by any contemporaries of hers with first-hand knowledge of happenings at Monticello, or even by Madison Hemings himself, who presumably had only second-hand knowledge of his paternity — the allegation of Jefferson's paternity of Sally Hemings' children appears to have originated with these 1873 newspaper stories.[101]

Then there is the following breathtaking statement by the late Eyler Robert Coates Sr. in his rebuttal to the Thomas Jefferson Memorial Foundation report: "Of course, all of this happened years before Madison was even born, at a time when he could not possibly know the facts he was relating of his own knowledge. Therefore, his evidence was little more than gossip."[102]

There is little or nothing to distinguish these contemporary attacks from what was being written about Hemings in 1873: "The fact that Hemings claims to be the natural son of Jefferson does not convince the world of its truthfulness. He is not supposed to be a competent witness in his own behalf. He was no doubt present at the time of accouch[e]ment, but his extreme youth would prevent him from knowing all the facts connected with that important event."[103]

Motives, Scandalmongers

The plaintive cry of the Jefferson apologist is and always has been "Why are they saying such dreadful things about Mr. Jefferson?" As we have seen, the motive in the case of black testifiers such as Madison Hemings is construed to be uppityness or its opposite, low self-esteem. Others who have attempted to bring the Hemings-Jefferson story to light are presented as one species or another of the politically motivated scandalmonger. The specific type of political motivation is not always the same. Prior to 1998, Jefferson's accusers were variously identified as, among other things, Federalists, abolitionists, southerner-haters, and scoundrels motivated by personal animus. Some of these identifications were correct, at least in part. For example, James Callender, who was the first to publish the Hemings-Jefferson story, was an unsavory character who created a niche for himself by printing scandalous stories about Founding Fathers. On the other hand, he also had a way of being substantially correct in what he wrote. The truth can be told by a scoundrel and still be the truth.

Similarly, S. F. Wetmore, who interviewed Madison Hemings and Israel Jefferson, has been charged with cynically manipulating both these men as a way of pursuing his carpetbagger agenda of drumming up sympathy for freedmen in the wake of the Civil War and with supplying most, if not all, of the material that was published as their first-person accounts. Again, these accusations are true, up to a point. Wetmore was an advocate for freedmen, a Maine man, the recipient of federal patronage, and a Republican activist in heavily Democratic, antiblack southern Ohio. His interviews with Hemings and Jefferson probably do contain a lot of boilerplate background material that he himself provided. It is worth noting, however, that Dumas Malone himself identified Wetmore's interview technique as one he developed and used in writing biographical sketches of both white and black subjects.[104] Moreover, it is a mistake to expect a newspaper interview from the 1870s to read like one from last week's *New York Times*. As George Juergen points out, reviewing a book on nineteenth-century journalism, "Through the Jacksonian era and after, editors defined news primarily in political terms and saw it as an instrument to serve party interests."[105] No one would claim that every nineteenth-century interview written to serve a political agenda should be discounted. For the Jefferson apologists, however, the political agenda of this particular interviewer and the identity of his subjects render these two particular interviews null and void.

Surely the most strident response to Wetmore's interview with Israel Jefferson came from Thomas Jefferson Randolph, a grandson of the third president, who issued a fierce rebuttal in a letter to the *Pike County Republican*. In addressing what he labeled a "calumny generated in the hotbed of party malice," Randolph asked rhetorically what could possibly be motivating the rumormongers. He then answered his own question with another question: "Can it be that they felt the necessity of pandering to a ferocious hate of the southern white man — which devours with depraved appetite every invention of calumny, and every circulation of malignity that can blacken or degrade his character[?]"[106]

Tale-telling Negroes and the scandalmongers who spread their unthinkable stories in order to pursue their own political agenda — this is how the pre-DNA Jefferson apologists defined the opposition. They devised a variety of defenses that could be brought into play singly or together. For the black testifiers who kept the story alive, the blame lay with issues of self-image. They were motivated by either a ludicrous overestimation of their own worth or a pitiful need to elevate themselves by telling lies. For those who publicized the story, the blame lay with an unscrupulous devotion to whatever political agenda they could be identified with. They were Federalists, or they were abolitionists or some other species of Negro-lover, or they just purely despised southerners. After the DNA test results appeared, Jefferson's enemies began to be characterized somewhat differently and the blame for threatening the great man's reputation reassigned to some extent. But the threat, it seemed, was greater than ever. In the words of John H. Works, the former president of the Monticello Association, "Defending Thomas Jefferson . . . has come to mean defending what America means."[107]

Satan Redux

In the post-DNA era the Jefferson apologists have identified three fresh avatars of Satan to explain the new impetus of the Hemings-Jefferson story: political correctness, multiculturalism, and historical revisionism. Underlying their continuing hostility is a racist and reactionary angst that extends well beyond the reputation of

Jefferson himself to include anxiety about how the history of the American republic as a whole is to be written and evaluated. This type of narrow-mindedness can be seen in some of the responses to the work of the Pulitzer Prize–winning historian Alan Taylor.

In the introduction to his survey *American Colonies* Taylor observes that "to write a history of colonial America used to be easier because the human cast and the geographic stage were both considered so much smaller. Until the 1960s, most American historians assumed that 'the colonist' meant English-speaking men confined to the Atlantic seaboard. Women were there as passive and inconsequential helpmates. Indians were wild and primitive peoples beyond the pale: unchanging objects of colonists' fears and aggressions. African slaves appeared as unfortunate aberrations in a fundamentally upbeat story of Englishmen becoming freer and more prosperous by colonizing open land."[108] Taylor's description of the peopling and colonizing of early America is reasonable, fair, and comprehensive. He deals with gender, race, politics, and economic opportunity. The analysis of the settlement of North America moves the story beyond an earlier narrative in which the continent was represented as a *terra nullius,* or "land belonging to no one," that was conquered and settled by white men.[109] Taylor's scholarship reflects an awareness that the early history of the United States was part of a worldwide system of colonial settler expansion involving the dispossession and genocide of indigenous peoples and the enslavement of Africans to develop the new land's wealth. White men did not do this alone; they were accompanied by white women, whose labor contributed to the colonies' growth, wealth, and development.

For people trained in graduate school since the 1960s, this is an accurate and reasonable assessment of the American past. Unfortunately, this view is not shared by some readers of American history. One reviewer on Amazon.com labels the book "a politically correct history of America before 1776." Taylor's synthesis is "a slur on the generations of historians that precede Taylor," the reviewer says.[110] I cite this review because it captures a widespread feeling in America today that the history being written and taught by some American historians and teachers is not objective or fair to the American past. In a 1998 Public Agenda survey more than "800 parents, including 200 immigrant parents, all with children in school" indicated that they all favored a more "traditional" history. What these parents wanted was an American history constructed around "conventional ideals and stories of what it meant to be an American." This history, the parents thought, should emphasize "the history of our Founding Fathers, and how this country was created."[111] What I have been suggesting in this essay about the American past probably would be dismissed by the parents referred to here as obscene, unthinkable, or politically correct.

The term *politically correct* is a cliché deployed to dismiss historical scholarship that deviates from a tradition of historical writing supporting "the idea of the nation as a continuous narrative of national progress."[112] The use of the phrase reflects the fact that, as Dirk Moses has written, "all modernizing societies comprise factions within their intelligentsia that struggle with one another to impose an authoritative interpretation of political and cultural reality on their respective public spheres. In this rivalry for cultural capital — prestige and influence — they deploy an arsenal of rhetorical devices to discredit the opposition and enhance their own position in the public-intellectual field."[113]

Using the phrase *politically correct* in public debate, the post-DNA Jefferson apologists now conjure up a fictive golden age when American history was objective, universalistic, and not particularistic — a lost era when there was no "politicization of American history."[114] Just when this was is not clear. As Elizabeth Clark writes, all history is "driven by the problems and questions set by the historian."[115] History is never apolitical. On the contrary, it is, as Keith Jenkins says, "always for someone."[116] I think this is what the scholar Reinhart Koselleck meant when he observed that "the discipline of history always performs a political function, albeit a changing one."[117] The pre-DNA history written about Jefferson and Hemings, to which the apologists now look back nostalgically, was in fact a history for white Americans only. It told whites who they were and who they were not by constructing a past unmarked by racial intermixture. To borrow a phrase from Mark Twain, this was "chloroform in print," an anesthetic designed to blot out the place of race, slavery, and sex in Jefferson's world and, more broadly, in the national myth.[118]

Recognition of this fact explains the current hostility on the part of post-DNA apologists to revisionist assessments of the relationship between Hemings and Jefferson. Their position reflects a rather naive understanding of the writing of history. In fact, the white people who have written the post-DNA critiques remind me of the Afrocentrists I have written about elsewhere.[119] Like the Afrocentrists, they have an unsophisticated idea of historical scholarship. History, they believe, is about great men, a pleasant and uncomplicated tale unmarked by either contingencies or disjunctures, a narrative both uplifting and teleological. History for these people, regardless of their color, is a chronicle of origins. If for the Afrocentrists their moment of glory was ancient Egypt, for the partisans of Jefferson it was the early republic, a time untroubled by black people who now "passionately want their families' oral traditions somehow validated by widespread acceptance of the Jefferson paternity thesis as historical fact."[120]

The post-DNA critics see those who now affirm a relationship between Jefferson and Hemings as advocates of "feel-good history" driven by "radical multiculturalism and postmodernism — which have . . . undermined traditional standards [of] objectivity in historical scholarship." Multiculturalism and postmodernism (which we can redefine as the latest wave of revisionist historiography) have unleashed a whole host of evils, according to critics of the

"Jefferson-Hemings paternity claim," which extend their malign influence far beyond the particulars of how we read Jefferson's own story.[121] The hostility to both of these intellectual trends is, at its heart, a reaction to the decentering of white Americans as the central agents of American history.

We hear this in college classrooms in California when white undergraduates question whether the history of Asians, blacks, Mexicans, or Native Americans is American history. The history of these people and the history of women are often deemed marginal and not central to an understanding of the American past. Why should we be surprised, then, that the reexamination of Thomas Jefferson's relationship to Sally Hemings has produced a reaction that borders on the risible? If there ever was a time when Americans and historians agreed about their past, it was a fictive past created to assuage the feelings of the dominant. The Asian, black, Mexican, and Native American understandings of America and its history were never the same as that of the white majority. I therefore have reservations about Peter Novick's idea that there was a "collapse of comity" in the historical profession in the 1960s.[122]

But was this comity or comedy? If comity is grounded in the idea of reciprocity, that is, the recognition by one group of people of the validity of their peers' ideas, then the study of American history in the 1940s and 1950s was not characterized by comity. There could be no exchange of ideas between the participating parties in a profession dominated by white men, as the American historical profession was before the 1960s, because the history written during this time excluded the ideas, actions, and experiences of racial minorities and women. These groups were largely invisible, silent, and thought to be unworthy of study. When, for example, Arthur Schlesinger Jr. wrote *The Age of Jackson*,[123] what dialogue was he engaging in with black people in a book that pretty much ignored the slavery issue?

Schlesinger's monograph was a celebration of the political triumph of white yeoman farmers; the fact that Jacksonian politics was based on slavery was not discussed. That is not to say that I think Schlesinger was a racist. This particular book, however, epitomizes those silences in the production of history that I referred to previously. As a first-year graduate student at Berkeley in 1967, I read Schlesinger's powerful essay "A Note on Historical Sentimentalism" and wondered if this was by the same person who had written *The Age of Jackson*.[124]

Arthur Schlesinger was a revisionist, an honorable participant in the intellectual tradition that informs the rethinking of early American history. So were J. C. Furnas, Pearl M. Graham, and Winthrop Jordan, all of whom specifically addressed the Hemings-Jefferson issue in the 1950s and 1960s, and Fawn Brodie, whose controversial 1974 book about Jefferson brought the Hemings relationship to the forefront of public consciousness and provoked bitter opposition from the Jefferson defenders.[125] Merrill Peterson dismissed Brodie's book by saying that "no serious student of Jefferson has ever declared his belief in it."[126] And Virginius Dabney, in a book intended as a refutation of Brodie, described Jefferson as "one of the principal historical victims of the current orgy of debunking."[127]

Unfortunately for Dabney and others like him, the revisionist "orgy" has continued. The civil rights movement, the women's movement, the rise of ethnic and cultural studies, immigration from Asia and Latin America, and the study of sexuality continue to diversify the history profession. The recent work of scholars such as Andrew Burstein, Martha Hodes, Kirsten Fischer, Annette Gordon-Reed, Joshua Rothman, and John Sweet, who are part of a larger revision and reconceptualization documenting the nation's mixed racial past, has moved beyond the silences and denials that characterized the work of earlier generations of American historians.[128]

As the great Oscar Wilde once observed, "The one duty we owe to history is to rewrite it."[129] But the Jefferson apologists see the reexamination of the Jefferson-Hemings relationship as something bad, and never more so than in the wake of the DNA revelations. "Historical revisionism is perfectly legitimate when it rests on a careful reassessment of the past. But what is presented as revision in this case is based on misleading headlines in the journal *Nature*, scientific evidence that was interpreted unscientifically, and conclusions in the media that have no basis in actual scientific fact."[130] According to two of its critics, the DNA information was presented to the American public in the manner of "a fascist or Stalinist propaganda machine."[131]

On issues concerning race in American historical scholarship, revisionism has been, for the most part, a force for progress and change. Certainly no one but an intellectual troglodyte would want to return to Ulrich B. Phillips's racist interpretation of slavery or John Burgess's white supremacist reading of Reconstruction. The 1998 DNA revelation was not a step backward in historical understanding or an example of totalitarian propaganda. Nor was it a "politically correct" version of the Nazis' "big lie."[132] It was an effort to create a more inclusive understanding of the American past, one that placed the history of the American republic and the plantation South in the history of the plantation complex, where amalgamation/miscegenation was commonplace.

The efforts of a new generation of American historians whose lives were shaped by the social movements of the 1960s and the Vietnam War have given the writing of American history a complexity and depth that earlier work in the field lacked. This revisionism has placed the history of America in a world context that an earlier emphasis on the English origins of the United States lacked. It is the movement away from that older history, with its emphasis on white people and the exclusion of Native Americans, blacks, and women, that has unsettled some white Americans. They no longer know whether the American history written in the second half of the twentieth century and the first decade of the twenty-first century is the history of the country in which they were born. What these white people must do is "stop viewing history as a plot against [them]."[133]

To read the post-DNA discussion about Thomas Jefferson and Sally Hemings is to confront an obsession focused on the question, Who are we? Jefferson can remain an American hero only if he never slept with a black woman. Yet if Thomas Jefferson is removed from the pantheon of white American heroes, then what is America? Is this a white nation, or was it a mongrelized one at the moment of its creation? How will the United States represent itself in the family of nations in the future? Will George and Martha Washington continue to be the nation's founding parents, or will they be replaced by Thomas Jefferson and Sally Hemings, or some other mixed-race couple, in the twenty-first century? What, in brief, is the public face of America to be, given the current debates about who or what is an American?[134] As the *Economist* recently observed, "Across the world, approaches to the teaching of children about their nation's past are hotly contested — especially at times of wider debates on national identity."[135] The debate about Thomas Jefferson and Sally Hemings has always been about national identity or who we are. This was true in the nineteenth and twentieth centuries, and it will continue to be true well into the twenty-first.

Given the equation of Jefferson with America and his affair with Hemings, I think their union has a symbolic significance that extends beyond most acts of amalgamation and miscegenation. Jefferson's central place in American national identity has created a problem for people who want to think of him as the father of a white nation and who feel that they alone have "the cultural authority to shape the public memory of the American past."[136] We can see this in the recent spate of books about the Founding Fathers.[137] More than history, these books are also a way of reassuring some white Americans that this is still a white-ruled country. Moreover, the post-DNA response to the 1998 revelation has to be placed in the context of a reactionary rewriting of southern history that has been going on since the Civil War.[138] This can be seen in the proliferation of racist and reactionary books, all intended to correct the errors of so-called politically correct history and most of them dealing with issues in southern history.[139]

No problem seems to be more unsettling to the champions of the "Lost Cause" than the issue of slavery. "As a collective idea and an emotional necessity," Wolfgang Schivelbusch has observed, "the idea of the formulation of the Lost Cause [was] a program for the conservation of national identity."[140] The postbellum idea of southern nationhood was built on the notion that pre–Civil War white southern society had been the victim of a Yankee juggernaut that had destroyed the institution that made the South distinctive, slavery. What white southerners erroneously called their peculiar institution was the defining characteristic of a lost paradise. This was what Margaret Mitchell meant in *Gone with the Wind* when she described the South as a civilization. All pasts are imagined, but some are more so than others. Central to the idea of the South as a nation was the institution of Negro slavery.

Slavery was a racial institution in the South from the 1640s until 1865. It was not like slavery in the ancient world, where slaves came from all classes and racial groups. It requires an extremely perfervid imagination to claim, as Walter D. Kennedy does, that "in the nineteenth century, white men were sold into slavery, black men owned slaves, and Native Americans owned black and red slaves."[141] The most interesting part of this quotation is the assertion that white men were sold into slavery. Initially, both whites and blacks served as indentured servants, but as racial lines hardened and slavery began to be seen as the answer to the southern colonies' chronic labor shortages, black bondspeople replaced whites as the permanent labor force of the South. It is true that blacks owned slaves, but most of these slaves were family members who could not be freed.[142] As for Native Americans owning slaves, this idea is not new to anyone familiar with the work of James Brooks and Theda Perdue.[143] The importance of this revisionist strategy resides in the fact that white southerners and other whites who feel victimized by blacks can now have the pleasure of knowing that they have slave ancestors too. History, rather than being an exercise devoted to the study of particulars, in this analytic strategy becomes an exercise in equivalences. This is a clever but not substantive rewriting of American history. The claim that whites were slaves creates a functional equivalent between black slavery and indentured servitude that did not exist. If whites were slaves, why were they not given that appellation? Why was the term *slave* reserved solely for blacks? The answer is simple. The idea of a white slave would have contradicted the racial assumption on which American Negro slavery rested, namely, that all slaves were black and all blacks were slaves. The idea of a free Negro under slavery was an anomaly. This exercise in white victim envy is reminiscent of the Afrocentrist claim that slavery was a holocaust. Slavery was many things; a holocaust it was not. In white America the popularity of this nonsense suggests that some white southerners and those who sympathize with them are nostalgic for a more comfortable past.

It also indicates that the ongoing controversy surrounding Thomas Jefferson and Sally Hemings is, to borrow a line from Fitzhugh Brundage, "emblematic of the continuing dialectic between black and white pasts in the present-day South."[144] Some white southerners still "bridle at blacks" being thought of as southerners or having anything to do with the Founding Fathers.[145] This explains, for example, the Monticello Association's opposition to the black Hemings's being buried in the Jefferson family graveyard. One member of the association is alleged to have said that "he had no interest in associating with Hemings' descendents in this life — or in death."[146] There is to be no intrusion of black southerners into some white southern space, even in death.

The opposition of some whites to the revelation that Thomas Jefferson fathered black children constitutes a form of *resentiment* directed at blacks for staking a claim on what was previously thought of as a white icon. This hostility raises questions about the United States' being color blind and challenges the comfortable notion that race is no longer an important marker of status in American society. Within the South and the United States at large, race may not have the importance that it had in Jefferson's day or before the civil rights movement, but it is still salient. It continues to occupy a prominent place in American politics, just as it continues to play an important role in American life.

The continuing contretemps surrounding Thomas Jefferson and Sally Hemings reveals something about how some white Americans, both southern and northern, want to think about the past. What they seem to want is a "color-blind" past in which both slavery and amalgamation/miscegenation are somehow erased. Arthur Schlesinger cautioned Americans about denying their past when he wrote that "history is to the nation as memory is to the individual. As a person deprived of memory becomes disoriented and lost, not knowing where he has been or where he is going, so a nation denied a conception of its past will be disabled in dealing with its present and its future."[147] This is why the Thomas Jefferson and Sally Hemings affair needs to be affirmed rather than denied.

Notes

Introduction

1. Ron Chernow, *Alexander Hamilton* (New York, 2004), 529. See also Annette Gordon-Reed, *Thomas Jefferson and Sally Hemings: An American Controversy* (Charlottesville, VA, 1997).

2. In the twentieth century, the most forceful defenders of Jefferson's reputation have been historians and Jeffersonophiles. See, e.g., Douglass Adair, "The Jefferson Scandals," in *Fame and the Founding Fathers,* ed. Trevor Colbourn (Indianapolis, 1974), excerpted at http://www.pbs.org/wgbh/pages/frontline/shows/jefferson/cron/1960scandal.html; Virginius Dabney, *The Jefferson Scandals* (New York, 1981); Dumas Malone, *Jefferson and His Time,* vols. 1, *Jefferson the Virginian* (Boston, 1948), and 4, *Jefferson the President, First Term, 1801–1805* (Boston, 1970); Alf J. Mapp Jr., *Thomas Jefferson, Passionate Pilgrim* (Lanham, MD, 1991); John Chester Miller, *The Wolf by the Ears* (New York, 1977); Merrill D. Peterson, *The Jefferson Image in the American Mind* (New York, 1962); and Willard Sterne Randall, *Thomas Jefferson: A Life* (New York, 1993).

3. Winthrop D. Jordan, *White over Black: American Attitudes toward the Negro, 1550–1812* (Chapel Hill, NC, 1968), 466.

4. Two books that chart the joys and pitfalls of interracial sex in the 1960s are Hettie Jones, *How I Became Hettie Jones* (New York, 1990); and Mark D. Naison, *White Boy: A Memoir* (Philadelphia, 2002). See also Anatole Broyard's memoir, *Kafka Was the Rage: A Greenwich Village Memoir* (New York, 1993); this book, which deals with Bohemian life and interracial sex in Greenwich Village in the 1940s, indicates that what became public in the 1960s was developing in the 1940s.

5. For these changes, see John D'Emilio and Estelle B. Freedman, *Intimate Matters: A History of Sexuality in America* (New York, 1998).

6. Fawn M. Brodie, *Thomas Jefferson: An Intimate History* (New York, 1974); Barbara Chase-Riboud, *Sally Hemings* (New York, 1979). A masterful and insightful essay about the reaction to these two wom-

en's works and what historians and others have said about Thomas Jefferson and Sally Hemings is Scot A. French and Edward Ayers, "The Strange Career of Thomas Jefferson: Race and Slavery in American Memory, 1943–1993," in *Jeffersonian Legacies,* ed. Peter S. Onuf (Charlottesville, VA, 1993), 418–57. Another thoughtful analysis of the historical debate about Jefferson and Hemings is Francis D. Cogliano, *Thomas Jefferson* (Charlottesville, VA, 2006), chap. 6.

7. French and Ayers, "Strange Career of Thomas Jefferson," 440.

8. See Brodie, *Thomas Jefferson,* 296; and Gordon-Reed, *Thomas Jefferson and Sally Hemings,* 195–96.

9. French and Ayers, "Strange Career of Thomas Jefferson," 427.

10. Ibid.

11. Garry Wills, "Uncle Thomas's Cabin," *New York Review of Books,* 18 April 1974, 26–28.

12. Jan Ellen Lewis and Peter S. Onuf, eds., *Sally Hemings and Thomas Jefferson: History, Memory, and Civic Culture* (Charlottesville, VA, 1999), 1. For the DNA evidence, see Eugene A. Foster, M. A. Jobling, P. G. Taylor, P. Donnelly, P. deKnijff, Rene Mierement, and C. Tyler-Smith, "Jefferson Fathered Slave's Last Child," *Nature* 196 (5 November 1998): 27–28. See also Eric S. Lander and Joseph J. Ellis, "Founding Father," ibid., 13–14.

13. See Andrew Burstein, *Jefferson's Secrets* (New York, 2005); Lewis and Onuf, *Sally Hemings and Thomas Jefferson;* Peter S. Onuf, *Jefferson's Empire: The Language of American Nationhood* (Charlottesville, VA, 2000); Joshua D. Rothman, *Notorious in the Neighborhood: Sex and Families across the Color Line in Virginia, 1787–1861* (Chapel Hill, NC, 2003); and John Wood Sweet, *Bodies Politic: Negotiating Race in the American North, 1730–1830* (Baltimore, 2003).

14. Philip D. Curtin, *The Rise and Fall of the Plantation Complex: Essays in Atlantic History* (Cambridge, 1990), ix.

15. Robin Blackburn, *The Making of New World Slavery* (New York, 1997), 309.

16. Ibid.

17. Joel Williamson, *New People* (New York, 1980), xiii.

18. Ira Berlin, *Many Thousands Gone: The First Two Centuries of Slavery in North America* (Cambridge, MA, 1998), introduction.

19. Winthrop D. Jordan, "American Chiaroscuro: The Status and Definitions of Mulattoes in the British Colonies," *William and Mary Quarterly* 19 (April 1962): 183–200.

20. Richard Hofstadter, *America at 1750: A Social Portrait* (New York, 1973), 115.

21. "Thomas Jefferson and Sally Hemings: Discovering and Dealing with the Truth," A Richmond Quest 2000 Symposium, Richmond, VA, 18 April 2000.

22. For the debate about Malinche and Cortés, see Frances Karttunen, "Rethinking Malinche," in *Indian Women of Early Mexico,* ed. Susan Schroeder, Stephanie Wood, and Robert Haskett (Norman, OK, 1997), 291–311.

23. Marilyn Grace Miller, *Rise and Fall of the Cosmic Race* (Austin, 2004), 23.

24. See Sylvia Fry, *Water from the Rock* (Princeton, NJ, 1991); François Furstenberg, *In the Name of the Father: Washington's Legacy, Slavery, and the Making of a Nation* (New York, 2006); Gary B. Nash, *The Forgotten Fifth: African Americans in the Age of Revolution* (Cambridge, MA, 2006); David Waldstreicher, *Runaway America* (New York, 2004); and Henry Wieneck's superb *An Imperfect God: George Washington and the Creation of America* (New York, 2003).

One | Sexuality

1. Philip D. Curtin, *The Rise and Fall of the Plantation Complex: Essays in Atlantic History* (Cambridge, 1990), ix.

2. For the distinction between "societies with slaves" and "slave societies," see M. L. Bush, *Servitude in Modern Times* (Cambridge, 2007), 16–17. See also Keith Bradley, *Slavery and Society at Rome* (Cambridge, 1994), 12–14.

3. Jeffrey Weeks, *Making Sexual History* (Cambridge, 2000), 7.

4. See, e.g., Ira Berlin, *Many Thousands Gone: The First Two Centuries of Slavery in North America* (Cambridge, MA, 1998), chap. 1; C. R. Boxer, *Race Relations in the Portuguese Colonial Empire, 1415–1825* (Oxford, 1963); Trevor Burnard, "The Sexual Life of an Eighteenth-Century Jamaican Slave Overseer," in *Sex and Sexuality in Early America,* ed. Merril D. Smith (New York, 1998), 171–72; John D. Garrigus, *Before Haiti: Race and Citizenship in French Saint-Domingue* (New York, 2006), chap. 2; Frances Gouda, *Dutch Culture over Seas* (Amsterdam, 1991), 163; Ramon A. Gutierrez, *When Jesus Came, the Corn Mothers Went Away: Marriage, Sexuality and Power in New Mexico, 1500–1846* (Stanford, CA, 1991), 51; Bernard Moitt, *Women and Slavery in the French Antilles, 1635–1848* (Bloomington, IN, 2001); Phillip D. Morgan, "Three Planters and Their Slaves: Perspectives on Slavery in Virginia, South Carolina, and Jamaica, 1750–1790," in *Race and Family in the Colonial South,* ed. Winthrop D. Jordan and Sheila L.

Skemp (Jackson, MS, 1987), 68 and 74; idem, "Interracial Sex in the Chesapeake and the British World, ca. 1700–1820," in *Sally Hemings and Thomas Jefferson: History, Memory, and Civic Culture,* ed. Jan Ellen Lewis and Peter S. Onuf (Charlottesville, VA, 1999), 72; Magnus Morner, *Race Mixture in the History of Latin America* (Boston, 1967); Robert C.-H. Shell, "The Tower of Babel: The Slave Trade and Creolization at the Cape, 1652–1834," in *Slavery in South Africa: Captive Labor on the Dutch Frontier,* ed. Elizabeth A. Eldredge and Fred Morton (Boulder, CO, 1994), 24; Megan Vaughan, *Creating the Creole Island* (Durham, NC, 2005); Owen White, *Children of the French Empire: Miscegenation and Colonial Society in French West Africa, 1895–1960* (Oxford, 1999), chap. 1; and Stephanie Wood, "Sexual Violation in the Conquest of the Americas," in Smith, *Sex and Sexuality in Early America,* 9–34.

5. For an insightful discussion of the evolution of the term *miscegenation,* see Elise Lemire, *"Miscegenation": Making Race in America* (Philadelphia, 2002), 4. In this book I use *mixed-race* and *interracial* except where I want to emphasize the full connotations of *amalgamation* and *miscegenation.*

6. Quoted in Boxer, *Race Relations,* 31, 16, 21.

7. Quoted in C. R. Boxer, *Salvador de Sa' and the Struggle for Brazil and Angola, 1602–1686* (Bristol, UK, 1952), 23.

8. Quoted in Boxer, *Race Relations,* 15.

9. Boxer, *Salvador de Sa',* 23.

10. Ibid.

11. Edward Long, *History of Jamaica,* vol. 2 (1774; New York, 1972), 327.

12. Ibid., 328. See also Winthrop D. Jordan, "American Chiaroscuro: The Status and Definition of Mulattoes in the British Colonies," *William and Mary Quarterly* 19 (April 1962): 183–200, an excellent study of the regional variations in British sexual mores in Britain's New World colonies.

13. Lee Edelman, *Homographesis* (New York, 1994), 44.

14. Laura Stoler, *Carnal Knowledge and Imperial Power* (Berkeley and Los Angeles, 2002), 80.

15. Jacquelyn Kilpatrick, *Celluloid Indians: Native Americans and Film* (Lincoln, NE, 1999), 63.

16. The legislation is quoted in Matthew Fry Jacobson, *Whiteness of a Different Color: European Immigrants and the Alchemy of Race* (Cambridge, MA, 1998), 22. For Jefferson's legislation, see Thomas Jefferson, *The Papers of Thomas Jefferson* (Princeton, NJ, 1950), 2:476–78.

17. Leon Litwack, *North of Slavery* (Chicago, 1961), 31.

18. David Theo Goldberg, *The Racial State* (New York, 2002), 104.

19. Both David Roediger and Noel Ignatiev err in tracing the emergence of white racial consciousness to the appearance of the white working class in the 1840s. Whiteness as a form of identity was present much earlier in American society. See David Roediger, *The Wages of Whiteness* (New York, 1991); and Noel Ignatiev, *How the Irish Became White* (New York, 1995). For Herrenvolk Democracy, see Pierre van den Berghe, *Race and Racism* (New York, 1967), 29.

20. Ibrahim Sundiata, *Brothers and Strangers: Black Zion, Black Slavery, 1914–1940* (Durham, NC, 2003), 25.

21. Rogers M. Smith, *Civic Ideals* (New Haven, CT, 1997), 167.

22. Samuel Sewall, *The Selling of Joseph: A Memorial,* ed. Sidney Kaplan (Amherst, MA, 1969), 10.

23. Sudipta Sen, *Distant Sovereignty: National Imperialism and the Origins of British India* (New York, 2002), chap. 5.

24. Quoted in Neil Foley, *The White Scourge* (Berkeley and Los Angeles, 1997), 22.

25. Quoted in Tony Horowitz, "Immigration and the Curse of the Black Legend," *New York Times,* 9 July 2006, 13.

26. Quoted in Randy Roberts, *Papa Jack* (New York, 1983), 154.

27. Etienne Balibar, "Racism and Nationalism," in *Race, Nation, Class: Ambiguous Identities,* by Etienne Balibar and Immanuel Wallerstein (New York, 1991), 40.

28. Verena Martinez-Alier, *Marriage, Class, and Colour in Nineteenth-Century Cuba,* 2nd ed. (Ann Arbor, 1989), xviii.

29. "Others within" is a paraphrase of the literary critic and comparativist Michele Wright in *Becoming Black* (Durham, NC, 2004), 7–8. For the origins of the concept, see Balibar, "Racism and Nationalism," 37–67.

30. Wright, *Becoming Black,* 8.

31. Andrew Burstein, *Jefferson's Secrets* (New York, 2005), 146.

32. See ibid.

33. For a discussion of some of the classical roots of Western racism, see Benjamin Isaac, *The Invention of Racism in Classical Antiquity* (Princeton, NJ, 2004).

34. David Bindman, *Ape to Apollo* (Ithaca, NY, 2002), 19.

35. Peter S. Onuf, *Jefferson's Empire: The Language of American Nationhood* (Charlottesville, VA, 2000), 169.

36. Ibid.

37. Stoler, *Carnal Knowledge and Imperial Power,* 80.

38. Blacks have this fear too, but it derives from a different context of power.

39. Thomas Jefferson, *Notes on the State of Virginia,* intro. Thomas Perkins Abernethy (New York, 1964), 175.

40. Thomas Jefferson, *Thomas Jefferson's Writings* (New York, 1984), 1098.

41. John M. Murrin, "The Jeffersonian Triumph and American Exceptionalism," *Journal of the Early Republic* 20 (Spring 2000): 1–25.

42. For insightful discussions of this process, see Winthrop D. Jordan, *White over Black: American Attitudes toward the Negro, 1550–1812* (Chapel Hill, NC, 1968); Litwack, *North of Slavery;* Gary B. Nash, *The Forgotten Fifth: African Americans in the Age of Revolution* (Cambridge, MA, 2006), chap. 3; John Wood Sweet, *Bodies Politic: Negotiating Race in the American North, 1730–1830* (Baltimore, 2003); and David Waldstreicher, *In the Midst of Perpetual Fetes* (Chapel Hill, NC, 1997).

43. Waldstreicher, *In the Midst of Perpetual Fetes,* 302.

44. Jefferson, *Notes on the State of Virginia,* 155.

45. *Colored American,* 30 September 1837.

46. On *Integrationsideologie,* see Albert S. Linderman, *The Jew Accused* (Cambridge, MA, 1991), 75.

47. Joyce Appleby, *Thomas Jefferson* (New York, 2003), xvi.

48. Severn Duvall, *"Uncle Tom's Cabin:* The Sinister Side of the Patriarchy," in *Images of the Negro in American Literature,* ed. Seymour L. Gross and John Hardy (Chicago, 1966), 163–80.

49. My understanding of how the closet operates has been expanded by conversations with Mike Sherry and by reading David Van Leer, "A View from the Closet: Reconcilable Differences in Douglass and Melville," in *Frederick Douglass and Herman Melville: Essays in Relation,* ed. Samuel Otter and Robert Levine (Chapel Hill, NC, 2008), 279–94.

50. John Gabriel Stedman, *Stedman's Surinam: Life in an Eighteenth-Century Slave Society,* ed. Richard Price and Sally Price (Baltimore, 1992), 93.

51. For one edition of this diary, see Douglas Hall, *In Miserable Slavery: Thomas Thistlewood in Jamaica, 1750–86* (London, 1989). See also Trevor Burnard, *Mastery, Tyranny, and Desire: Thomas Thistlewood and His Slaves in the Anglo-Jamaican World* (Chapel Hill, NC, 2004), 217; Morgan, "Three Planters and Their Slaves"; and idem, "Interracial Sex."

52. Quoted in James Hugo Johnson, *Race Relations in Virginia and Miscegenation in the South, 1776–1860* (Amherst, MA, 1970), 167.

53. Michel Foucault, *The History of Sexuality,* vol. 1 (New York, 1978), 38.

54. For an insightful discussion of the flouting of this prohibition against sex with blacks, see Joshua D. Rothman, *Notorious in the Neighborhood: Sex and Families across the Color Line in Virginia, 1787–1861* (Chapel Hill, NC, 2003).

55. Stedman, *Stedman's Surinam,* xxxiii.

56. Quoted in John Chester Miller, *The Wolf by the Ears* (New York, 1977), 163. See also Rothman, *Notorious in the Neighborhood,* 4, 12–13.

57. Richard Godbeer, *Sexual Revolution in Early America* (Baltimore, 2002), 201.

58. Ibid.

59. David B. Davis, *In the Image of God* (New Haven, CT, 2001), 7. See also John Dollard, *Caste and Class in a Southern Town* (New York, 1949), 144.

60. For George Wythe's alleged relationship with the slave woman Lydia Broadnax, see Morgan, "Interracial Sex." For a different interpretation of this relationship, see Carolyn Jean Powell, "What's Love Got to Do with It? The Dynamics of Desire, Race, and Murder in the Slave South" (PhD diss., University of Massachusetts, Amherst, 2002), chap. 4.

61. See Douglass Adair, "The Jefferson Scandals," in *Fame and the Founding Fathers,* ed. Trevor Colbourn (Indianapolis, 1974), 227–73, excerpted at http://www.pbs.org/wgbh/pages/frontline/shows/jefferson/cron/1960scandal.html; Virginius Dabney, *The Jefferson Scandals* (New York, 1981); Dumas Malone, *Jefferson and His Time,* vols. 1, *Jefferson the Virginian* (Boston, 1948), 4, *Jefferson the President, First Term, 1801–1805* (Boston, 1970), and 6, *The Sage of Monticello* (Boston, 1981); Alf J. Mapp Jr., *Thomas Jefferson, Passionate Pilgrim* (Lanham, MD, 1991); Miller, *Wolf by the Ears;* Merrill D. Peterson, *The Jefferson Image in the American Mind* (New York, 1962); Willard Sterne Randall, *Thomas Jefferson: A Life* (New York, 1993); and Douglas Wilson, "Thomas Jefferson and the Character Issue," *Atlantic Monthly,* November 1992, 62. See also Sander Gilman, *Sexuality: An Illustrated History* (New York, 1989), 101.

62. Ronald Walters, *The Antislavery Appeal* (Baltimore, 1976), 74.

63. Nathan I. Huggins, "The Deforming Mirror of the Truth," in *Revelations: American History, American Myths,* ed. Brenda Smith Huggins (New York, 1995), 253.

64. Ibid., 277.

65. Benjamin Braude, comment delivered at "Collective Degradation: Slavery and the Construction of Race" conference, Yale University, New Haven, CT, 7–8 November 2003.

66. Quoted in Itabari Njeri, *The Last Plantation* (Boston, 1977), 171.

67. Jefferson, *Notes on the State of Virginia*, 133.

68. Quoted in Lawrence W. Levine, *Black Culture and Black Consciousness* (New York, 1977), 288.

69. Two informative interpretations of the whys of this relationship are Annette Gordon-Reed, *Thomas Jefferson and Sally Hemings: An American Controversy* (Charlottesville, VA, 1997), 109, 156–57; and Rothman, *Notorious in the Neighborhood,* chap. 1.

70. E. Hoetink, *Caribbean Race Relations* (New York, 1976), 120.

71. Quoted in Miller, *Wolf by the Ears,* 164.

72. For an informative discussion of *Lost Boundaries,* see Gayle Wald, *Crossing the Line* (Durham, NC, 2000), chap. 3. See also Thomas Cripps, *Making Movies Black* (New York, 1969), 226–32. Cripps's book also contains interesting discussions of both versions of *Imitation of Life,* on pp. 10, 209, 255, and 270, and of *Pinky,* on pp. 221, 232–40, and 249.

73. Joanne Pope Mellish, "Playing Whoop and Hide," *Reviews in American History* 30 (June 2002): 249.

74. Here I paraphrase a question asked by Barbara J. Fields in her influential essay "Ideology and Race in American History," in *Region, Race, and Reconstruction,* ed. J. Morgan Kousser and James McPherson (New York, 1982), 149.

75. Jefferson, *Notes on the State of Virginia*, 138.

76. Quoted in Jordan, *White over Black,* 173.

77. Long, *History of Jamaica,* 2:321.

78. Quoted in Fawn M. Brodie, *Thomas Jefferson: An Intimate History* (1974; repr., New York, 1998), 433.

79. The best discussion of the place of mulattoes in the British Atlantic world is in Jordan, *White over Black,* 167–78; for Jamaica's special place in this context, see 176–78.

80. Jefferson, *Thomas Jefferson's Writings,* 1345.

81. Daniel Coker, "A Dialogue between a Virginian and an African Minister," in *Negro Protest Pamphlets,* ed. Dorothy Porter (New York, 1969), 29.

82. Dollard, *Caste and Class,* 143.

83. Jordan, *White over Black,* 138.

84. Jefferson, *Thomas Jefferson's Writings,* 1115.

85. Onuf, *Jefferson's Empire,* 46.

86. Anthony F. C. Wallace, *Jefferson and the Indians* (Cambridge, MA, 1999), 95.

87. Quoted in Richard Godbeer, "Eroticizing the Middle Ground: Anglo-Indian Sexual Relations along the Eighteenth-Century Fron-

tier," in *Sex, Love, Race: Crossing Boundaries in North American History,* ed. Martha Hodes (New York, 1999), 94.

88. William Byrd, *Histories of the Dividing Line betwixt Virginia and North Carolina* (1841; New York, 1967), 120.

89. On this point, see the discussion of Native Americans in Jeffersonian Virginia in Miller, *Wolf by the Ears,* 67.

90. Barbara J. Fields, "Of Rogues and Geldings," *American Historical Review* 108 (2003): 1004.

91. Gary B. Nash, *The Unknown American Revolution* (New York, 2005), 116–17.

92. For a discussion of Daniel Coker's racial origins, see Ira Berlin, *Slaves without Masters* (New York, 1974), 281; and Gary B. Nash, *Forging Freedom* (Cambridge, MA, 1998), 232. The phrase *heterosexual closet* as I use it describes more than a place of hiding; it refers to a vantage point from which one looks out, watching as well as watched.

93. Nash, *Unknown American Revolution,* 115.

94. Ibid.

95. Quoted in Paul Finkelman, *Slavery and the Founders,* 2nd ed. (New York, 2000), 138–39.

96. Long, *History of Jamaica,* 2:328–29.

97. Quoted in Nicholas Spice, "Tomorrow It'll All Be Over," *London Review,* 25 May 2006.

98. W. E. B. Du Bois, *The Souls of Black Folk* (1903; New York, 1961), 15.

99. Franz Fanon, *Black Skin, White Masks* (New York, 1967), 47.

100. Hayden White, "The Forms of Wildness: Archeology of an Idea," in *Tropics of Discourse* (Baltimore, 1978), 178.

101. Alexis de Tocqueville, *Democracy in America,* ed. J. P. Mayer (New York, 1967), 317.

102. White, "Forms of Wildness," 178.

103. Patricia Williams, "Rush Limbaugh's Inner Black Child," *Nation,* 27 October 2003, 11.

104. Wald, *Crossing the Line,* ix.

105. Henry Wiencek, *An Imperfect God: George Washington and the Creation of America* (New York, 2003), 78.

106. Gilberto Freyre, *The Masters and the Slaves* (1946; New York, 1956), 279.

107. See Miller, *Wolf by the Ears,* 179.

108. Ibid., 178. See also Jon Kukla, *Mr. Jefferson's Women* (New York, 2007), which makes it clear that Jefferson liked sex and the company of women.

109. Quoted in Joseph J. Ellis, *American Sphinx: The Character of Thomas Jefferson* (New York, 1997), 305. Since writing these words, Professor Ellis has come to accept the possibility that Thomas Jefferson was Sally Hemings's lover and probably the father of her children. See idem, "Jefferson Post DNA," *William and Mary Quarterly,* 3rd ser., 57 (January 2000): 125–38.

110. Arnold I. Davidson, *The Emergence of Sexuality* (Cambridge, MA, 2001), 53.

111. Ibid.

112. Jefferson, *Notes on the State of Virginia,* 134.

113. Brenda Stevenson, *Life in Black and White* (New York, 1996), 141.

114. Lloyd A. Thompson, *Romans and Blacks* (Norman, OK, 1989), 108.

115. Quoted in Peter Biller, "The Black in Medieval Science: What Significance?" (paper presented at "Collective Degradation: Slavery and the Construction of Race" conference, Yale University, New Haven, CT, 7–8 November 2003).

116. See Jordan, *White over Black,* 32–43, quotation from 34; for a comparable discussion of African women, see 35. See also Gilman, *Sexuality,* 101–2; and David M. Friedman, *A Mind of Its Own: A Cultural History of the Penis* (New York, 2001), 107–13.

117. Gilman, *Sexuality,* 101.

118. Long, *History of Jamaica,* 2:328.

119. Foucault, *History of Sexuality,* 1:38.

120. See Wright, *Becoming Black,* 27.

121. Quoted in Cynthia H. Burton, *Jefferson Vindicated* (Keswick, VA, 2005), 110–11.

122. See *Oxford Classical Dictionary,* 3rd ed., rev., s.v. "Valeria Messal(l)ina."

123. Hannah Cullwick, *The Diaries of Hannah Cullwick,* ed. Liz Stanley (New Brunswick, NJ, 1984). For a more expansive reading of the diaries, see Anne McClintock, *Imperial Leather* (New York, 1995), 75–180.

124. Stanley, introduction to Cullwick, *Diaries,* 7.

125. Hillary McD. Beckles, *Centering Women: Gender Discourses in Caribbean Slave Society* (Princeton, 1999), 41.

126. Quoted in Vaughan, *Creating the Creole Island,* 156.

127. Stanley, introduction to Cullwick, *Diaries,* 13.

128. For a discussion of this underworld, see Steven Marcus, *The Other Victorians* (New York, 1964); Judith R. Walkowitz, *Prostitution and Victorian Society* (Cambridge, 1980); idem, *City of Dreadful Delight*

(Chicago, 1992); and Jeffrey Weeks, *Sex, Politics, and Society* (London, 1981).

129. Paul Robinson, *Gay Lives* (Chicago, 1999), xi.

130. This is the view propounded by Saidiya V. Hartman in *Scenes of Subjection* (Oxford, 1997), 79–90.

131. Weeks, *Making Sexual History*, 60.

132. Sharon Block, "Sexual Violence, Violent Sex: Constructions of Rape in Early America" (paper presented at the conference "Violence in Early America," McNeil Center for Early American Studies, Philadelphia, October 2001), 25.

133. For a history of the penis, see Friedman, *Mind of Its Own*.

134. For the transformation in thinking about women's sexuality, see Nancy F. Cott, "Passionlessness," in *Heritage of Her Own*, ed. Nancy F. Cott and Elizabeth H. Pleck (New York, 1997), 162–82.

135. The quotation is from Hartman, *Scenes of Subjection*, 85.

136. Kathleen Brown, *Good Wives, Nasty Wenches, and Anxious Patriarchs* (Chapel Hill, NC, 1996), 237.

137. Beckles, *Centering Women*, 40.

138. Quoted in Ann Twinam, *Public Lives, Private Secrets* (Stanford, CA, 1999), 9.

139. Harriet Jacobs, *Incidents in the Life of a Slave Girl*, ed. Jean Fagan (Cambridge, MA, 1987), 55–56.

140. Ibid., 54.

141. Ibid., 55.

142. Stephanie M. H. Camp, "Sally Hemings and Thomas Jefferson," *Mississippi Quarterly* 53 (2000): 276.

143. Rothman, *Notorious in the Neighborhood*, 38.

144. Wald, *Crossing the Line*, 110.

145. Suzanna Sawyer, "Bobbittizing Texaco: Dis-Membering Corporate Capital and Re-Membering the Nation in Ecuador," *Cultural Anthropology* 17 (2002): 152.

146. Mieko Nishida, *Slavery and Identity* (Bloomington, IN, 2003), 1. For examples of the model, see John W. Blassingame, *The Slave Community* (New York, 1972); and Herbert Gutman, *The Black Family in Slavery and Freedom, 1750–1925* (New York, 1976). Ira Berlin's *Generations* (Cambridge, MA, 2003) constitutes an important break with this paradigm.

147. For some interesting but dated discussions of slave culture, see the following works: Blassingame, *Slave Community*; Eugene D. Genovese, *Roll Jordan Roll* (New York, 1972); Gutman, *Black Fam-*

ily; Levine, *Black Culture and Black Consciousness*; George Rawick, *The American Slave: A Composite Autobiography* (Westport, CT, 1972); and Sterling Stuckey, *Slave Culture: Nationalist Theory and the Foundations of Black America* (New York, 1987). An article that is not often cited but is very important in the construction of the idea of a slave culture is idem, "Through the Prism of Folklore: The Black Ethos in Slavery," in *Going through the Storm: The Influence of African American Art in History* (New York, 1994).

148. Herbert Aptheker, *The Negro People in America* (New York, 1946), 62.

149. For the problem of betrayal in a slave revolt, see James Sidbury, *Ploughshares into Swords* (New York, 1997), chap. 3. See also William W. Freehling, *The Road to Disunion* (New York, 1990), 81.

150. Nishida, *Slavery and Identity*, 1.

151. Ibid., 5.

152. Jefferson, *Notes on the State of Virginia*, 138.

153. Hillary McD. Beckles, *Natural Rebels* (New Brunswick, NJ, 1989), 67.

154. Ibid.

155. Robert C. H. Shell, *Children of Bondage: A Social History of the Slave Society at the Cape of Good Hope, 1652–1838* (Hanover, NH, 1994), 287.

156. Ibid., 288.

157. Quoted in Freyre, *Masters and the Slaves*, 83.

158. Maria de los Reyes Castillo Bueno, *Reyita* (Durham, NC, 2000), 166.

159. Burnard, *Mastery, Tyranny, and Desire*, 217.

160. See, e.g., Charles W. Chesnutt, *The Wife of His Youth* (1899; Ann Arbor, 1968); idem, *The House behind the Cedars* (1900; New York, 1969); Nella Larsen, *Passing* (New York, 1929); James Weldon Johnson, *The Autobiography of an Ex-Colored Man* (1912; New York, 1990); Philip Roth, *The Human Stain* (New York, 2000); and Wallace Thurman, *The Blacker the Berry* (New York, 1929).

161. Oliver Cromwell Cox, *Caste, Class, and Race* (New York, 1959), 360.

162. Miller, *Wolf by the Ears*, 164.

163. Quoted in Lelia Moritz Schwarcz, *The Spectacle of the Races* (New York, 1993), 128.

164. On this point, see A. J. R. Russell-Wood, *The Black Man in Slavery and Freedom in Colonial Brazil* (Oxford, 1982), 10.

165. Ibid.

166. Quoted in Jeffrey D. Needell, "Identity, Race, Gender, and Modernity in the Origins of Gilberto Freyre's Oeuvre," *American Historical Review* 100 (1995): 66.

167. Quoted in Howard Winant, *The World Is a Ghetto* (New York, 2001), xxix.

168. Freyre, *Masters and the Slaves,* 279.

169. Ibid., 5.

170. Ulrich Bonnell Phillips, "Southern Negro Slavery: A Benign View," in *American Negro Slavery: A Modern Reader,* ed. Allen Weinstein and Frank Otto Gatell, 2nd ed. (New York, 1968), 68.

171. Peter Wade, *Blackness and Race Mixture* (Baltimore, 1993), 10.

172. Ibid., 11–17. On this problem of mixed-race nationality, see also Alexander S. Dawson, *Indian and Nation in Revolutionary Mexico* (Tucson, 2004); Colin M. MacLachlan, *The Forging of the Cosmic Race* (Berkeley and Los Angeles, 1990); Thomas Skidmore, *Black into White* (Durham, NC, 1983); and José Vasconcelos, *The Cosmic Race* (Baltimore, 1979). For an insightful critique of Vasconcelos's book, see Marilyn Grace Miller, *Rise and Fall of the Cosmic Race* (Austin, 2004).

173. Anthony D. Smith, *National Identity* (London, 1991), 11.

174. Hodes, *Sex, Love, Race.*

175. Joel Williamson, *New People* (New York, 1980), xii.

Two | Character and History, or "Chloroform in Print"

The phrase "Chloroform in Print" is taken from Mark Twain, *Roughing It* (1872; Berkeley and Los Angeles, 1993), 107.

1. See an interview with Gore Vidal, 24 April 2006, http://www.pbs.org/jefferson/archives/interviews/Vidal.htm.

2. Roland Barthes, *Mythologies,* trans. Annette Lavers (New York, 1972), 143.

3. François Furstenberg, *In the Name of the Father: Washington's Legacy, Slavery, and the Making of a Nation* (New York, 2006), 20.

4. Ibid., 22 and chaps. 2 and 5.

5. Quoted in Clarence E. Walker, "The American Negro as Historical Outsider, 1836–1935," in *Deromanticizing Black History: Critical Essays and Reappraisals* (Knoxville, TN, 1991), 91.

6. Quoted in Russ Castronovo, *Fathering the Nation: American Genealogies of Slavery and Freedom* (Berkeley and Los Angeles, 1995), 15.

7. Nathan I. Huggins, "The Deforming Mirror of Truth," in *Revelations: American History, American Myths,* ed. Brenda Smith Huggins (New York, 1995), 256.

8. Quoted in Leon Litwack, *Trouble in Mind* (New York, 1998), 2005.

9. Bain Attwood, *Telling the Truth about Aboriginal History* (Crows Nest, New South Wales, 2005), 15.

10. Quoted in ibid., 17.

11. Michel-Rolph Trouillot, *Silencing the Past* (Boston, 1995), 26.

12. Tony Judt, "What Was the Cold War?" *New York Review of Books,* 23 March 2006, 15.

13. Hector St. John de Crevecoeur, *Letters from an American Farmer* (1782; New York, 1982), 37.

14. Charles Austin Beard and Mary Ritter Beard, *The Rise of American Civilization* (New York, 1927), 1:15.

15. Castronovo, *Fathering the Nation,* 13.

16. Milton M. Gordon, *Assimilation in American Life* (New York, 1964), 104–14.

17. Ibid., 115.

18. See Nicholas D. Kristof, "Is Race Real?" *New York Times,* 11 July 2003, A19.

19. See Benjamin Quarles, *Black Abolitionists* (New York, 1969), 219.

20. Quoted in John Chester Miller, *The Wolf by the Ears* (New York, 1977), 63.

21. Harriet Jacobs, *Incidents in the Life of a Slave Girl* (1861; Cambridge, 1987), 19.

22. Elaine K. Ginsberg, ed., *Passing and the Fictions of Identity* (Durham, NC, 1996), 4.

23. Quoted in Ellen Fitzpatrick, *History's Memory* (Cambridge MA, 2002), 75.

24. Ibid., 24.

25. George Fredrickson, *The Black Image in the White Mind* (Middletown, CT, 1971), chap. 6.

26. For examples of the incorporation of mixed-race children into black families, see June Cross, *Secret Daughter* (New York, 2006); Ely Green, *An Autobiography* (Athens, GA, 1990); Anne Moody, *Coming of Age in Mississippi* (New York, 1968); and Gregory Howard Williams, *Life on the Color Line* (New York, 1995). For a similar course of events in a white family, see Henry Wiencek, *An Imperfect God: George Washington, His Slaves, and the Creation of America* (New York, 2003), 282–90.

27. Quoted in John Hope Franklin and Loren Schwengier, *In Search of*

the Promised Land: A Slave Family in the Old South (New York, 2006), 18.

28. Nikita A. Foston, "Strom Thurmond's Black Family," *Ebony,* March 2004, 162–66. See also Thurmond's black daughter's memoir: Essie Mae Washington-Williams and William Stadiem, *Dear Senator: A Memoir by the Daughter of Strom Thurmond* (New York, 2005).

29. Quoted in Washington-Williams and Stadiem, *Dear Senator,* 135.

30. "Thurmond Family Struggles with Different Truth," *New York Times,* 20 December 2003, A1.

31. Ira Berlin, *Generations* (Cambridge, MA, 2003), 199.

32. "Thurmond Family Struggles with Different Truth."

33. See Clarence E. Walker, "Denial Is Not a River in Egypt," in *Sally Hemings and Thomas Jefferson: History, Memory, and the Civic Culture,* ed. Jan Ellen Lewis and Peter S. Onuf (Charlottesville, VA, 1999), 195.

34. *Encyclopædia Britannica Online,* s.v. "Johnson, Richard M.," http://www.britannica.com/ib/article9043867 (accessed 28 June 2007). See also "Marriage Extraordinary," *Lexington Observer and Kentucky Reporter,* 29 November 1832, which deals with the marriage of "Thomas W. Scott, a white man, to Miss Adeline J. Johnson, a mulatto girl and reputed or acknowledged daughter of the Honorable Richard M. Johnson, one of the representatives of the State of Kentucky in the Congress of the United States."

35. There are a number of wonderful and useful books on whiteness. I think the best one for understanding the creation of whiteness as ideology is Matthew Fry Jacobson, *Whiteness of a Different Color: European Immigrants and the Alchemy of Race* (Cambridge, MA, 1998).

36. By post-DNA literature I mean books written after 1998. See, e.g., Cynthia H. Burton, *Jefferson Vindicated* (Keswick, VA, 2005); Eyler Robert Coates Sr., *The Jefferson-Hemings Myth: An American Travesty* (Charlottesville, VA, 2001); Rebecca L. McMurry and James F. McMurry Jr., *Anatomy of a Scandal: Thomas Jefferson and the Sally Story* (Shippensburg, PA, 2002); Thomas F. Sheehan, comp., *Thomas Jefferson / Sally Hemings: Two Hundred Years of Controversy* (Keswick, VA, 1998); and Robert F. Turner, ed., *Report of the Scholars Commission on the Jefferson-Hemings Matter,* online at http://www.tjheritage.org/scholars.html.

37. See Eugene Foster, M. A. Jobling, P. G. Taylor, P. Donnelly, P. de-Knijff, Rene Mierement, and C. Tyler-Smith, "Jefferson Fathered Slave's Last Child," *Nature* 196 (5 November 1998): 27–28. Two sources that show that historians can accept the DNA evidence are Joseph J. Ellis, "Jefferson Post DNA," *William and Mary Quarterly,* 3rd ser., 57

(January 2000): 125–38; and Winthrop D. Jordan, "Hemings and Jefferson: Redux," in Lewis and Onuf, *Sally Hemings and Thomas Jefferson*, 35–51. See also Fraser D. Neiman, "Coincidence or Casual Connection? The Relationship between Thomas Jefferson's Visits to Monticello and Sally Hemings's Conceptions," *William and Mary Quarterly*, 3rd ser., 57 (January 2000): 198–210.

38. Quoted in the interview with Gore Vidal cited in n. 1, above.

39. Scot A. French, *The Rebellious Slave* (Boston, 2004), 5. The concept of unthinkable history appears in Trouillot, *Silencing the Past*, 73.

40. Benedict Anderson, *Imagined Communities: Reflections on the Origin and Spread of Nationalism* (London, 1983), 136.

41. See Douglass Adair, "The Jefferson Scandals," in *Fame and the Founding Fathers*, ed. Trevor Colbourn (Indianapolis, 1974), chap. 8, excerpted at http://www.pbs.org/wgbh/pages/frontline/shows/jefferson/cron/1960scandal.html; Dumas Malone, *Jefferson and His Time*, vols. 1, *Jefferson the Virginian* (Boston, 1948), 4, *Jefferson the President, First Term, 1801–1805* (Boston, 1970), and 6, *The Sage of Monticello* (Boston, 1981); Alf J. Mapp Jr., *Thomas Jefferson, Passionate Pilgrim* (Lanham, MD, 1991); Miller, *Wolf by the Ears*; Merrill D. Peterson, *The Jefferson Image in the American Mind* (Charlottesville, VA, 1998); and Willard Sterne Randall, *Thomas Jefferson: A Life* (New York, 1993).

42. Annette Gordon-Reed, *Thomas Jefferson and Sally Hemings: An American Controversy* (Charlottesville, VA, 1997), xii.

43. Miller, *Wolf by the Ears*, 177.

44. Malone, *Jefferson and His Time*, vol. 4, *Jefferson the President, First Term, 1801–1805*, 214. In fairness to Malone, he does note that Jefferson was "not a plaster saint and incapable of moral lapses" (ibid.). This statement would explain Jefferson's attempted affair with his neighbor's wife, Mrs. John Walker, before he was married. It does not shed light on the affair with Hemings, which lasted thirty-eight years and thus would hardly qualify as a "lapse." For a complete discussion of the Walker affair, see ibid., 446–51.

45. Dumas Malone, address to the Monticello Association, Keswick Hunt Club, Keswick, VA, 2 May 1976, http://www.monticello-assoc.org/articles/Malone%20Talk.html.

46. Ellen Randolph Coolidge to Joseph Coolidge, 24 October 1858, http://www.pbs.org/wgbh/pages/frontline/shows/jefferson/cron/1858ellenlett.html.

47. Henry S. Randall to James Parton, 1 June 1868, http://www.pbs.org/wgbh/pages/frontline/shows/jefferson/cron/1868randall.html.

48. Michel Foucault, *Language, Counter-Memory, Practice,* ed. Donald F. Bouchard (Ithaca, NY, 1977), 156–57.

49. Gail Hawkes, *Sex and Pleasure in Western Culture* (Malden, MA, 2004), 140.

50. Ibid.

51. William Byrd II, *The Commonplace Book of William Byrd II of Westover,* ed. Kevin Berland, Jan Kristen Gilliam, and Kenneth L. Lockridge (Chapel Hill, NC, 2001), 67.

52. See Miller, *Wolf by the Ears,* 179.

53. Sigmund Freud, *Leonardo da Vinci and a Memory of His Childhood,* trans. Alan Tyson, 1st American ed. (New York, 1964), 19.

54. Ibid., 80.

55. Henry Abelove, *Deep Gossip* (Minneapolis, MN, 2003), 32.

56. Malone, *Jefferson and His Time,* vol. 4, *Jefferson the President, First Term, 1801–1805,* 214.

57. See ibid.

58. Miller, *Wolf by the Ears,* 168. For a brilliant and illuminating discussion of the white Jeffersons' stake in the Hemings affair, see Jan Ellen Lewis, "The White Jeffersons," in Lewis and Onuf, *Sally Hemings and Thomas Jefferson,* 127–60, a remarkable analysis of the inner workings of a family and its complicity in the process of denial.

59. Quoted in Mary Chestnut, *Mary Chestnut's Civil War, 1861–1865,* ed. C. Vann Woodward (New Haven, CT, 1981), 169.

60. Randall to Parton, 1 June 1868.

61. Ellen Randolph Coolidge to Joseph Coolidge, 24 October 1858.

62. Randall to Parton, 1 June 1868.

63. Ellen Randolph Coolidge to Joseph Coolidge, 24 October 1858.

64. Michael Haneke, interview, *Cache,* DVD, directed by Michael Haneke (Culver City, 2005).

65. Cynthia A. Kierner, *Scandal at Bizarre: Rumor and Reputation in Jefferson's America* (New York, 2004).

66. Guido Ruggiero, *The Boundaries of Eros* (New York, 1985), 151–52.

67. Wiencek, *An Imperfect God,* 84.

68. Ibid., 84–85.

69. On lynching, see Philip Dray, *At the Hands of Persons Unknown* (New York, 2000); and James H. Madison, *A Lynching in the Heartland: Race and Memory in America* (New York, 2001).

70. Quoted in Lee Edelman, *Homographesis* (New York, 1994), 43.

71. Haneke, interview.

72. Randall to Parton, 1 June 1868.

73. Ellen Randolph Coolidge to Joseph Coolidge, 24 October 1858.

74. Brian Connolly, e-mail message to author, 22 January 2007.

75. *The Lustful Turk* (1828; New York, 1983). For an interesting discussion of this novel, see Steven Marcus, *The Other Victorians* (New York, 1964), 196–216.

76. Mapp, *Thomas Jefferson*, 34.

77. Adair, "Jefferson Scandals."

78. Thomas Jefferson Heritage Society Web site, http://www.tjheritage .org/index.html.

79. The Jefferson apologist Herbert Barger, of the Thomas Jefferson Heritage Society, makes an unconvincing case that the Randolph name was in play prior to release of the DNA results. See http:// www.angelfire.com/va/TJTruth/randolph.html.

80. Madison Hemings, interview by S. F. Wetmore, *Pike County Republican*, March 1873, online at http://www.pbs.org/wgbh/pages/ frontline/shows/jefferson/cron/1873march.html.

81. John A. Jones, editorial in *Waverly Watchman*, 18 March 1873, quoted with permission from Dumas Malone and Steven H. Hochman, "A Note on Evidence: The Personal History of Madison Hemings," *Journal of Southern History* 41 (November 1975): 523–28, online at http://www.pbs.org/wgbh/pages/frontline/shows/jefferson/ cron/1873rebuttal.html.

82. Israel Jefferson, interview by S. F. Wetmore, *Pike County Republican*, December 1873, online at http://www.pbs.org/wgbh/pages/ frontline/shows/jefferson/cron/1873israel.html.

83. Thomas Jefferson Randolph, letter to the editor of the *Pike County Republican*, 25 December 1873, http://www.pbs.org/wgbh/pages/ frontline/shows/jefferson/cron/1873randolph.html.

84. Peterson, *Jefferson Image in the American Mind*, 187.

85. Quoted in Richard Hofstadter, *The Progressive Historians* (New York, 1968), 28.

86. Gordon-Reed, *Thomas Jefferson and Sally Hemings*, chap. 1.

87. See Eric Foner, *Who Owns History?* (New York, 2002).

88. James Baldwin, *Collected Essays* (New York, 1998), 382.

89. Annette Gordon-Reed, "Why Jefferson Scholars Were the Last to Know," 3 November 1998, http://www.samsloan.com/jeff-5.htm.

90. E. M. Halliday, *Understanding Thomas Jefferson* (New York, 2002), 168.

91. Kenneth Warren, *So Black and Blue* (Chicago, 2003), 9.

92. Quoted in Elizabeth A. Clark, *History, Theory, Text: Historians and the Linguistic Turn* (Cambridge, MA, 2004), 65.

93. Ibid.

94. Quoted in Theodore Rosengarten, *All God's Dangers: The Life of Nate Shaw* (New York, 1974), 109.

95. Ralph Ellison, *Invisible Man* (New York, 1947), 3.

96. Quoted in John Langston Gwaltney, *Drylongso: A Self Portrait of Black America* (New York, 1980), 29.

97. For some recent work on the historiography of black American history, see John Ernest, *Liberation Historiography* (Chapel Hill, NC, 2004); and Yaacov Shavit, *History in Black: African-Americans in Search of an Ancient Past* (Portland, OR, 2001). See also Walker, *Deromanticizing Black History,* chap. 5; and idem, *We Can't Go Home Again: An Argument about Afrocentrism* (New York, 2001), chap. 1.

98. Henry Louis Gates Jr., *Thirteen Ways of Looking at a Black Man* (New York, 1997), 106.

99. For examples of this genre, see William Wells Brown, *Clotel: or the President's Daughter: A Narrative of Slave Life in the United States,* ed. Robert S. Levine (Boston, 2000); and Barbara Chase-Riboud, *Sally Hemings* (New York, 1979).

100. Dwight McBride, *Why I Hate Abercrombie & Fitch* (New York, 2005), 4.

101. David N. Mayer, http://www.ashbrook.org/articles/mayer-hemings.html#IV.

102. Eyler Robert Coates Sr., http://www.angelfire.com/va/TJTruth/rebuttal.html.

103. Jones, editorial in *Waverly Watchman,* 18 March 1873.

104. Malone and Hochman, "Note on Evidence."

105. George Juergen, review of *The Commercialization of News in the Nineteenth Century,* by Gerald J. Baldasty, *American Historical Review* 99 (1994): 650.

106. Randolph to editor of the *Pike County Republican,* 25 December 1873.

107. Quoted in Coates, *Jefferson-Hemings Myth,* 12.

108. Alan Taylor, *American Colonies* (New York, 2001), ix.

109. Henry Reynolds, *The Law of the Land* (Ringwood, Australia, 1987), 12.

110. See Epops, review of *American Colonies,* by Alan Taylor, *Amazon Reviews,* 28 May 2007, 4. See also Gordon Wood, "Apologies to the Iroquois," review of *The Divided Ground: Indians, Settlers, and the Northern Borderland of the American Revolution,* by Alan Taylor, *New York Review of Books,* 6 April 2005. The phrase *politically correct* does not appear in this review, but Taylor's interpretation of relations between Native Americans and whites raises Wood's hackles.

111. John Pyne, "The Struggle for History at the Precollegiate Level," *Perspectives* 38 (May 2000): 26–27.

112. Homi K. Bhabha, *Narration and Nation* (New York, 1990), 4. For a discussion of the concept of political correctness, see John K. Wilson, *The Myth of Political Correctness* (Durham, NC, 1995).

113. A. Dirk Moses, "Revisionism and Denial," in *Whitewash: On Keith Windschuttle's Fabrication of Aboriginal History*, ed. Robert Manne (Melbourne, 2003), 338. A book that claims to "rescue real history from the politically correct memory hole" is Thomas Woods Jr., *The Politically Incorrect Guide to American History* (Washington, DC, 2004).

114. McMurry and McMurry, *Anatomy of a Scandal*, xii.

115. Clark, *History, Theory, Text*, 7.

116. Quoted in ibid., 22.

117. Quoted in ibid.

118. Mark Twain, *Roughing It* (1872; Berkeley and Los Angeles, 1993), 107.

119. See Walker, *We Can't Go Home Again*. On Afrocentrism, see also Molefi Kete Asante, *The Afrocentric Idea* (Philadelphia, 1987); and idem, *Afrocentricity* (Trenton, NJ, 1992). For other critiques of Afrocentrism, see Stephen Howe, *Afrocentrism* (New York, 1998); and Mary Lefkowitz, *Not Out of Africa* (New York, 1996).

120. David N. Mayer, quoted in McMurry and McMurry, *Anatomy of a Scandal*, xii.

121. Ibid., xiii.

122. Peter Novick, *That Noble Dream: The "Objectivity Question" and the American Historical Profession* (Chicago, 1988), chap. 13.

123. Arthur M. Schlesinger Jr., *The Age of Jackson* (Boston, 1945).

124. Arthur M. Schlesinger Jr., "A Note on Historical Sentimentalism," *Partisan Review* 16 (1949): 968–81.

125. Fawn M. Brodie, *Thomas Jefferson: An Intimate History* (New York, 1974).

126. Peterson, *Jefferson Image in the American Mind*, 186.

127. Virginius Dabney, *The Jefferson Scandals* (New York, 1981), 6.

128. See Andrew Burstein, *Jefferson's Secrets* (New York, 2005); Martha Hodes, ed., *Sex, Love, Race: Crossing Boundaries in North American History* (New York, 1999); Kirsten Fischer, *Suspect Relations* (Ithaca, NY, 2002); Gordon-Reed, *Thomas Jefferson and Sally Hemings*; Joshua D. Rothman, *Notorious in the Neighborhood: Sex and Families across the Color Line in Virginia, 1787–1861* (Chapel Hill, NC, 2003); and John Wood Sweet, *Bodies Politic: Negotiating Race in the American North, 1730–1830* (Baltimore, 2003).

129. Quoted in Arthur M. Schlesinger Jr., "History and National Stupidity," *New York Review of Books,* 27 April 2006, 14.

130. Coates, *Jefferson-Hemings Myth,* 9.

131. McMurry and McMurry, *Anatomy of a Scandal,* 7.

132. Ibid.

133. Vine DeLoria Jr., *Custer Died for Your Sins* (Norman, OK, 1996), 175.

134. For two reactionary statements about American nationality, see Patrick Buchanan, *State of Emergency: The Third World Invasion and Conquest of America* (New York, 2006); and Samuel P. Huntington, *Who Are We?* (New York, 2004).

135. "Where History Isn't Bunk," *Economist,* 17 March 2007, 64.

136. Scot A. French and Edward Ayers, "The Strange Career of Thomas Jefferson: Race and Slavery in American Memory, 1943–1993," in *Jeffersonian Legacies,* ed. Peter Onuf (Charlottesville, VA, 1993), 419.

137. For several examples of this genre, see Ron Chernow, *Alexander Hamilton* (New York, 2004); Joseph J. Ellis, *American Sphinx: The Character of Thomas Jefferson* (New York, 1997); idem, *Founding Brothers: The Revolutionary Generation* (New York, 2000); and David McCullough, *John Adams* (New York, 2001).

138. See the following fine books: David Blight, *Race and Reunion: The Civil War in American Memory* (Cambridge, MA, 2001); W. Fitzhugh Brundage, *The Southern Past* (Cambridge, MA, 2005); James C. Cobb, *A Way Down South* (New York, 2005); and Gaines Foster, *Ghosts of the Confederacy* (Oxford, 1987).

139. See James Ronald Kennedy and Walter Donald Kennedy, *The South Was Right!* (Gretna, LA, 2003); and Walter Donald Kennedy, *Myths of American Slavery* (Gretna, LA, 2003).

140. Wolfgang Schivelbusch, *The Culture of Defeat* (New York, 2003), 59.

141. Walter Donald Kennedy, *Myths of American Slavery,* 19. See also Steve Wilkins and Douglas Wilson, *Southern Slavery as It Was* (Moscow, ID, 1996).

142. See Luther Porter Jackson, *Free Negro Labor and Property Holding in Virginia, 1830–1860* (1942; New York, 1969); and Larry Kroger, *Black Slave Owners: Free Black Slave Masters in South Carolina, 1790–1860* (Jefferson, NC, 1985). On the perils of black slave ownership, see Michael P. Johnson and James L. Roark, *Black Masters* (New York, 1984).

143. See James F. Brooks, *Captives and Cousins* (Chapel Hill, NC, 2002); and Theda Perdue, *Slavery and the Revolution of Cherokee Society, 1540–1866* (Knoxville, TN, 1979).

144. Brundage, *Southern Past,* 317.

145. Ibid. Brundage used the words "bridle at blacks" to describe white Richmond's opposition to blacks' celebrating their emancipation on the grounds of the state capitol. The words can also be applied to white southern opposition to blacks' claiming to be descendants of Jefferson.

146. Lucian K. Truscott IV, "The Reunion Upon a Hill," *New York Times,* 16 July 2003, A3.

147. Schlesinger, "History and National Stupidity."

Index

Halliday, E. M., 83
Haneke, Michael, 75
Hawkes, Gail, 71–72
Hemings, Beverly, 37–38
Hemings, Eston, 5, 37–38
Hemings, Harriet, 37–38
Hemings, Madison, 4, 81–82, 86–88
Hemings, Mary, 48
Hemings, Sally, 30–31, 53, 77. *See also* Jefferson-Hemings affair
"Herrenvolk Democracy," 16–17
historical revisionism, 89, 92–95, 97–98
Hodes, Martha, 94
Hofstadter, Richard, 7
Howell, Samuel, 36–37
Huggins, Nathan, 29, 60
Human Stain, The (Roth), 37
hypodescent, law of, 28, 31

Ignatiev, Noel, 105n19
Imitation of Life (film), 31
indentured servitude, 6, 20, 97–98
India, 18
Integrationsideologie, 22–23
interracial sex: antimiscegenation laws and, 7, 19, 25, 36; case studies on confronting, 64–67; as "closeted" sex, 24–27; colonial experience and, 2, 13–15, 53; national identity and, 15–23, 28–29, 38–39, 53–55; as southern shortcoming, 28, 46; as transgression against whiteness, 42. *See also* master-slave relationships

Jacobs, Harriet, 24, 47, 64
Jamaica, 15, 37
Japan, 16
Jefferson, Israel, 81, 88

Jefferson, Martha Wayles, 30, 39, 72, 77
Jefferson, Randolph, 80–81
Jefferson, Thomas: citizenship limitations and, 16; on intermarriage with Native Americans, 34–35; *Notes on the State of Virginia*, 1, 8, 20, 30, 83; racial attitudes of, 1, 20–21, 30, 32–37, 42, 50; resettlement proposals of, 21–22; sexual appetite of, 39–41, 43, 70–72; slavery and, 22; as virtuous exemplar, 2, 23, 27–28, 68–69, 73, 96. *See also* Jefferson-Hemings affair
Jefferson-Hemings affair: contemporary comments on, 1–2, 42–43, 70, 74–75, 78–82, 88–89; DNA evidence of, 5, 8, 80–81, 95; historical analyses of, 3–6, 28, 68–71, 73–74, 80, 82–84, 86–87, 94; as national unifier, 29, 96–97; as romantic relationship, 23; scandalmonger (motives) and, 87–89; "somebody else did it" (defense) and, 78–81; unreliability of black testimony (defense) and, 81–87, 89; unthinkableness (defense) and, 68–74, 84; "white family would have known" (defense) and, 74–78
Jenkins, Keith, 91
Johnson, Richard M., 67
Jordan, Winthrop, 3–4, 7, 34, 40, 41, 94
Judt, Tony, 62
Juergen, George, 88

Kennedy, Walter D., 97
Kierner, Cynthia, 76
Koselleck, Reinhart, 92

Phillips, U. B., 54, 95
Pike County Republican, 81, 88
Pinky (film), 31
"plantation complex," 6, 13, 49
political correctness, 89–92
Portuguese colonies, 14
postmodernism, 92–93
Protestants, 14

racial states, definition of, 16
racism, discussions of, 85–86
Randall, Henry S., 70, 75, 78–79
Randall, Willard Sterne, 68
Randolph, Martha Jefferson, 75
Randolph, Richard, 76
Randolph, Thomas Jefferson, 70,
    74–75, 78–79, 81–82, 88–89
rapes, 8, 13, 45–46
Rawick, George, 49
reactionary historical revisionism,
    97–98
reasoned outcome arguments, 67,
    68, 82–83
Reed, Annette Gordon-. *See*
    Gordon-Reed, Annette
resettlement proposals, 21–22
revisionism. *See* historical
    revisionism
Reyita, 52
Robinson, Paul, 44–45
Rochefoucauld. *See* La
    Rochefoucauld-Liancourt,
    duc de
Roddenberg, Seaborn, 19
Roediger, David, 105n19
Roth, Philip, 37, 52
Rothman, Joshua, 5, 94
Ruggiero, Guido, 76
Russell-Wood, A. J. R., 54

Sawyer, Suzanna, 48
Sayre, Nathan, 66
scandalmongers, 87–89
Schivelbusch, Wolfgang, 97
Schlesinger, Arthur, Jr., 93–94,
    99
self-interest. *See* survival
    strategies
Sen, Sudipta, 18
Sewall, Samuel, 18
sexual desire, 33–34, 39–41, 71–72,
    80
sexual innocence/ignorance,
    76–77
Shaw, Nate, 84
Shell, Robert C. H., 51
"sleeping white." *See* survival
    strategies
Smith, Rogers, 17
social class. *See* class lines
social mobility, 48
South Africa, 16, 51
southern historiography, 97–98
Spanish colonies, 15
Stanley, Liz, 43
Stedman, John Gabriel, 24–25
Stevenson, Brenda, 41
Stoler, Laura, 21
Stowe, Harriet Beecher, 24
Stuckey, Sterling, 49
"Surinam marriage," 25–26
survival strategies, 45–48, 50–53
Sweet, John, 5, 94

Taney, Roger, 60
Taylor, Alan, 90–91
Thistlewood, Thomas, 24
Thomas, Mary, 51
Thomas Jefferson Heritage
    Society, 80